OUR LIFE WITH JESUS

OUR LIFE WITH JESUS

Faith and Life Series

BOOK THREE

Ignatius Press, San Francisco
Catholics United for the Faith, New Rochelle

Nihil Obstat: Rev. Msgr. Daniel V. Flynn, J.C.D.
                 Censor Librorum
Imprimatur: + Joseph T. O'Keefe, D.D.
                 Vicar General, New York

Director: Rev. Msgr. Eugene Kevane, Ph.D.
Assistant Director and General Editor: Patricia I. Puccetti, M.A.
Writer: Theresa Vorndran

Catholics United for the Faith, Inc., and Ignatius Press gratefully acknowledge the guidance and assistance of Reverend Monsignor Eugene Kevane, former Director of the Pontifical Catechetical Institute, Diocese of Arlington, Virginia, in the production of this series. The series intends to implement the authentic approach in Catholic catechesis given to the Church in the recent documents of the Holy See and in particular the Conference of Joseph Cardinal Ratzinger on "Sources and Transmission of Faith".

Excerpts from the Penny Catechism (Prow Books, Kenosha, WI, 1970). Excerpts from the Pius X Catechism of Christian Doctrine (Center for Family Catechetics, 1980).
Catholics United for the Faith and Ignatius Press are grateful for permissions to reprint copyrighted material.

Contents

1. God Loves Us 7
2. God Created the World.. 11
3. Learning about God 15
4. The Promise of a Savior 19
5. Abraham: The Father of God's People 23
6. The Prophet Moses... 27
7. King David 31
8. God's Laws of Love 35
9. Loving God Most of All 39
10. The Lord's Day 43
11. Obedience and Love 47
12. Purity and Truth 51
13. God's Tender Mercy... 57
14. Meeting Jesus in Confession 61
15. The Christ Child Is Born 67
16. Jesus Grows in Age and Wisdom 71
17. Signs and Wonders.. 75
18. The Last Supper, Our First Mass 79
19. Jesus Gives His Life for Us 83
20. Offering Gifts of Love 89
21. The Holy Mass 93
22. Offering Jesus to the Father 97
23. The Bread of Life 103
24. Jesus Comes to Us in the Holy Eucharist........................ 105
25. Jesus Rises in Splendor 111
26. The Coming of the Holy Spirit 117
27. God's Family on Earth 121
28. Our Life in the Church 125
29. Mary, Our Mother and Queen 131
30. The Communion of Saints 135
    Words to Know 139
    We Pray 145
    Art Credits 151

1   God Loves Us

Did you know that God has lived for ever? Close your eyes and imagine billions and billions of years ago. God was alive!

Now imagine billions of years stretching into the future. God will be just as all-powerful and alive. God is eternal, which means He had *no* beginning and He will *never* die. He is almighty, all-holy and all-wise. His power and beauty are infinite. That means they are far too great ever to be measured.

God was thinking of you, loving you, and wanting you from all eternity. Long before He put one star in the sky, He knew you. He knew your name. He knew your face. He knew the color of your eyes and the sound of your voice. You are very precious to Him. He could have made some other person, but He wanted you. So He made you just the way you are.

God loves you so much that He made you in His image. He made a part of you that, like Him, will never die. This part of you is called your soul. It is a spirit. You cannot see it. But your soul gives you the power to think and the power to love. With your soul, you can learn things, enjoy music and stories, talk, and laugh. Without your soul, you would be no more intelligent than a rock. Without your soul, you could never love anyone. When God made us in His image, He opened up many treasures for us.

Our best treasure is God Himself. He is always with us. He knows everything about us, even our thoughts. He loves us more than anyone else loves us. He gave us our soul so we could love Him in return. Sometimes this seems hard to do because we cannot see or hear God. God is pure spirit.

There is only one God, but in God there are three Persons: God the Father, God the Son, and God the Holy Spirit. Jesus, the Second Person of the Blessed Trinity, came to earth as a sign of God's love for us. Because Jesus, Who is God, became a man like us, it is easier for us to love Him. We know that He is gentle, kind, and good. He taught us to put God first. He taught us to obey God, even when we do not feel like it. He taught us that by loving each other, we give God glory and show our love to Him.

Jesus taught His apostles—and us—how to pray to the Heavenly Father. Sometimes He went out into the desert to pray. This showed us that it is good to take special times to be alone with God. Other times, Jesus prayed with a gathering of friends or a great multitude. We imitate Him when we pray with our family or classmates or others in our parish.

Once the apostles asked Jesus how to pray. He taught them a prayer that is still used in our Church. We hear it every time we go to Mass. It is called the "Our Father" or the Lord's Prayer:

Our Father Who art in Heaven, hallowed be Thy Name; Thy Kingdom come; Thy will be done on earth as it is in Heaven. Give us this day our daily bread, and forgive us our trespasses as we forgive those who trespass against us; and lead us not into temptation, but deliver us from evil. *Amen.*

In this prayer we praise God, we say we are sorry for our sins, we ask for His love and forgiveness, and we ask Him to watch over us. Prayer is talking with God. It is important to do it every day because it keeps us close to Him.

Words to Know:

infinite   prayer   all-perfect   create

Q. 1   *Who created us?*
God created us.

Q. 2   *What purpose did God have in mind when He created us?*
God created us to know Him, to love Him and to serve Him in this life, and then to be happy with Him for ever in the next life, in Heaven.

Q. 3   *Who is God?*
God is the all-perfect Being, Creator, and Lord of Heaven and earth.

Q. 4   *What does "all-perfect" mean?*
"All-perfect" means that every perfection is found in God, without defect and without limit; in other words, it means that He is *infinite* power, wisdom, and goodness.

Q. 5   *Does God have a body as we have?*
No, God does not have a body, for He is a perfectly pure spirit.

Q. 6   *Where is God?*
God is in Heaven, on earth, and in every place: He is the unlimited Being.

Q. 7 *Has God always existed?*
Yes, God always has been and always will be: He is the eternal Being.

Q. 8 *Does God know all things?*
Yes, God knows all things, even our thoughts: He is all-knowing.

Q. 9 *What is prayer?*
Prayer is a lifting of the soul to God to know Him better, to adore Him, to thank Him, to tell Him we are sorry, and to ask Him for what we need.

"I will never forget you. See, I have carved you on the palm of My hand."

(Isaiah 49:15—16)

2 God Created the World

In the beginning, there was only a great darkness. There was no earth, no light, no people or animals or trees.

God was perfectly happy, so He did not need to create these things. But in His infinite goodness and love, He wanted to share His life. So He created all of Heaven and earth.

Creating something means making it out of nothing. When a carpenter makes a chair, he cannot do it without his nails and hammer and wood. When a baker makes a cake, he cannot do it without eggs and sugar and milk. But God *created* the world, which means He made it out of nothing. Only God is so powerful that He can make something just by thinking of it and willing it to be.

First God said, "Let there be light!" and the sun and moon and millions of stars brightened the sky. Then He created the sparkling sea and the land. He put birds in the air and animals of all shapes and sizes on the earth. Finally, God made a man and a woman in His own image. They were Adam and Eve, our first parents. God made them to love and help each other and to rule the earth and enjoy its beauty together.

Everything that God created is good. We believe in God's wisdom and love because everything in nature has a purpose.

For example, a porcupine's funny needles are not for decoration. God planned them so that a porcupine could protect himself from danger.

A mother kangaroo's pouch is not an accident. God planned that soft, warm place to keep her babies safe.

The things in nature work together. When a bee takes food from a

12

flower, his legs get full of pollen which is needed for little flower seeds. As he flies away, the pollen scatters so lots of new flowers will grow.

God made the mountains tall so they can catch snow. Then the snow high above the ground melts slowly and trickles down to water the earth all year.

It takes a brilliant plan to make all of nature work this way. That is why we believe it comes from God.

God has a purpose for you, too. He created you to be happy in Heaven someday with Him. But He also created you to be a part of this world. He gave His life to your soul. He gave you talents to serve His Kingdom. He gave you five senses, so you can see, hear, taste, touch, and smell the beautiful things on this earth. Naturally, God wants you to enjoy these gifts and be happy.

Only one thing ruins His plan for our happiness. That is sin. When we sin, we do not use God's gifts in the way He intended us to use them. When we sin we do not feel right inside. We feel torn and upset. We turn our backs on our loving God.

God gave us our mind and will so we can live up to His plan for us. We can choose to do what is right and good. When we obey our parents, study well, are kind to our neighbors and friends, and respect animals and nature, we please God. We feel right inside.

To be happy for ever, we must get to Heaven. Heaven is our destiny. God promises He will take us there if we love and serve Him in this world. We will be completely happy in Heaven because we will see God face to face. We are not sure what Heaven looks like, but we know it will be even more beautiful than we can imagine. God gave us His word: "Eye has not seen, nor ear heard, nor the heart of man conceived, what God has prepared for those who love Him."

Q. 10 *Does God take care of created things?*
Yes, God takes care of created things and exercises *providence* over them; He preserves them in existence and directs all of them toward their own proper purposes with infinite wisdom, goodness, and justice.

Q. 11 *Can God do all things?*
God can do all that He wills to do: He is the all-powerful one.

Q. 12 *What does "Creator" mean?*
"Creator" means that God made all things out of nothing.

Q. 13 *What does "Lord" mean?*
"Lord" means that God is the absolute master of all things.

Words to Know:

Creator   Heaven   Lord

3   Learning About God

We believe God is with us because He gives us many signs of His presence. One of the best signs is the created world all around us. Even a person who has never heard about God can figure out that Someone very wise and powerful must have put nature together. Everything in nature acts for a purpose. It has order, and it has great beauty. The different parts of creation give us many clues about God, our Creator.

Mountains and vast forests reveal that our Creator is majestic and great. Oceans and rushing waterfalls tell us of His power. Fresh roses and sunsets reflect God's beauty. The growth and seasons of living things show us that God is wise. And the company of good, loving people teaches us more about God's own goodness and love.

God made sure we had many ways to discover Him, since He especially created us to know and love Him. Long ago, during the time the world waited for the coming of the Savior, God sent messages to His people on earth through holy men called prophets. Moses, for example, was a great prophet. Through Moses, and other Old Testament prophets, God taught mankind to be good, to stop sinning, and to trust in Him.

God later revealed Himself to us more directly through Jesus Christ, His Son, Our Savior. Remember, Jesus *is* God, so His way of life on earth showed us what God is really like. We learn through Jesus that God is gentle as well as just, slow to anger, rich in mercy, and full of love. We learn that He forgives the greatest sins if we are sorry for them. We learn that He is always ready to heal us, help us, and be our friend.

16

Jesus often taught these things through parables. Parables are stories about ordinary people that teach us something about the Kingdom of God. Each parable is different, but they all teach one clear message from God: "Love God with all your heart and soul and might, and love your neighbor as yourself."

We find Jesus' parables and other things He said and did in a big book called the Bible. The Bible has two parts, the Old Testament and the New Testament. The Old Testament teaches us about creation, our first parents, and the long wait and preparation of God's people for a Savior. The New Testament tells the story of Jesus and how the Church began. It teaches us that the Church is our ladder to Heaven.

God inspired holy men from earliest times to write down His laws and teachings. These are recorded in the Bible. That is why we call it the Word of God. We also call it the Scriptures. Scripture and Tradition teach us everything we need to know to live a good and happy life that is pleasing to God.

Jesus, our Teacher, once called Himself the Good Shepherd because He watches over us and leads us to the Father. After Jesus left the earth, He gave us another shepherd to take His place. We call this shepherd the Vicar of Christ or the Pope. The Pope teaches and guides the Church for Christ. He encourages us to become saints. He is the head of the bishops all over the world. He helps them in their special mission to help us keep learning and growing in our faith.

Words to Know:

Pope   bishop   Bible   Old Testament
New Testament   saint

Q. 14 *Can God do also something evil?*
No, God cannot do evil, because *He cannot will evil*, for He is infinite goodness. But He *tolerates* evil in order to leave creatures free, and He knows how to bring good even out of evil.

4 The Promise of a Savior

God made other creatures, besides us, who have the power to know and to decide. These creatures can think as we do, but they are much smarter and more powerful. They are called angels. We cannot see the angels because they are pure spirits. They have no bodies. But they are very real and alive, because God shared His life with them, too.

God created the angels out of love. He wanted them to be happy with Him in Heaven for ever. But He gave them the gift of free will so they could make a choice. Some of the angels chose to rebel against God. They refused to serve God.

The bad angels and the good angels fought a great battle. The good, obedient angels won because they had God and the truth on their side. God rewarded them with the joys and love of His Kingdom. Then He threw all the bad angels (devils) into Hell; they can never see God again because they locked themselves out of Heaven when they chose to rebel against Him.

Like the angels, Adam and Eve were given free wills. They were created for the everlasting joys of God's friendship, but they had a choice. God tested that choice. He told Adam and Eve to enjoy all the fruits of their rich, beautiful garden, except for the fruit of one tree. He warned them that if they ate this fruit, they would be very sad. They promised to obey God.

One day, however, the devil tricked Eve by lying to her. He told her that if she disobeyed God, she would be like Him. Eve believed the devil and broke her promise to God. Then she tempted Adam to break his promise, too. This first sin was called original sin. Since

EMISIT ADAM DE
PARADISO DS ET POSVIT CHERV
CVSTODE CVFLAMEO GLAD
ADAM

Adam was the father of all people on earth, the effects of his original sin carry on to all generations, including our own, and to each one of us.

When Adam and Eve disobeyed God, they were worried, sad, and full of fear. They lost the gift of His life in their souls. They could no longer please Him or be His friends. Worst of all, they had to suffer and die without any hope of Heaven.

God punished Adam and Eve, but He never stopped loving them. He planned a special way for them to come back to Him after their Fall. He promised a Savior, Who would make up for their sin and re-open the gates of Heaven. This promise became the light and hope of the People of God.

At the coming of the Savior, God gave His children a sacrament that pours God's life back into the soul, washing away original sin. This sacrament is called Baptism. When the priest poured the waters of Baptism over you, you were born into God's family. God came to live inside of you. You are able to go to Heaven someday.

You can keep your soul full of grace (God's life within us) by obeying and loving God. What happened to Adam and Eve teaches us that no matter how attractive a sin might appear, it is never worth the price. Sin makes us sad and afraid, and it hurts our friendship with God. Obedience and love make us happy, and they strengthen our friendship with God. If we keep growing in grace, we will one day rejoice with God in Heaven, our true home.

Words to Know:

sin   original sin   Baptism
Savior   the Fall

Q. 15 *What is sin?*
Sin is an offense done to God by disobeying His law.

Q. 16 *What is original sin?*
Original sin is the sin which mankind committed in Adam, its head, and which every human being receives from Adam through natural descent.

Q. 17 *How is original sin taken away?*
Original sin is taken away by Holy Baptism.

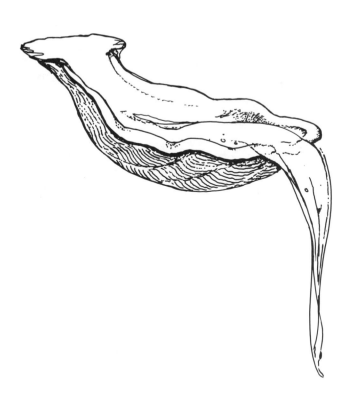

5 Abraham: The Father Of God's People

The people who lived after Adam and Eve waited hundreds and hundreds of years for the promised Savior. Some of them got tired of waiting and made up their own gods. They worshipped great things in nature that they could see, like fire, the moon, and the sun. They even worshipped objects they made with their hands, like animal statues made of gold.

These people forgot God, but God did not forget them. He remembered His promise. But first God chose certain faithful men to prepare the people for the coming of the Savior. Abraham was one of the first He chose. Abraham had great faith.

God asked Abraham to leave his home and friends and go on a long journey. Abraham did not understand clearly, but he believed in the one, true God, and he trusted Him. He took his wife Sarah, his nephew Lot, and all his flocks to a faraway country called Canaan. God rewarded Abraham for his obedience. He told him, "This land I will give to you. You shall be the father of a great people. Through you all nations will be blessed." Because of this promise, the land of Canaan was called "the Promised Land". Abraham did not realize it, but God's plan was that the Savior would be born from his family.

God was very good to Abraham. He gave him great riches and increased his flocks. But Abraham was worried because he had no children. Even though Abraham and his wife Sarah were very old, God blessed them with a child. They named the boy Isaac, which means laughter, since he was such a surprise and delight in their lives.

24

One day God tested Abraham to see if he loved Him above all else. He knew Isaac was more precious to Abraham than any other treasure. One night God said to Abraham, "Take Isaac and go to a mountain that I will show you. There offer Me your son as a sacrifice." Abraham's heart was breaking, but again he put God first. He trusted and obeyed Him. He cut wood for the sacrifice, took Isaac, and walked up into the mountains. Just as Abraham was about to strike his only son, an angel sent by God stopped him. "God now knows that you truly love Him," the angel said, "for you are ready to obey Him in all things. God is pleased with you. He will bless you even more."

Abraham was very glad. He picked up a ram which was caught in the bushes and sacrificed it in thanksgiving. Then the angel told Abraham that his family would be more numerous than the stars in the sky. He told him that out of his great people, God's Chosen People, the Savior of the world would one day be born.

God gave this great reward to Abraham and his children because Abraham always obeyed His voice, even when God asked him to do something very hard. Some day God may test us as He tested Abraham. He may ask us to give up something we love or want in order to follow His commands. This happens in small ways every day. God asks you to obey your mother right away, even though you would rather keep playing. God asks you to be kind to everyone, even people who have hurt you. God asks you to follow His laws, even when it would be easier to follow another way. God has happiness and blessings in store for your love and obedience, just as He did for His faithful servant Abraham.

Words to Know:

                faith   trust   Abraham

26

6   The Prophet Moses

As God promised Abraham, the Chosen People grew and multiplied like the stars in the sky. They spread across the land as a great and powerful people. Night and day, God watched over them and blessed them, for He loved them as His own children.

Sometimes God tests the very people He loves the most, and this happened to the Israelites in Egypt. They were God's special favorites, His chosen ones, but God allowed a long, dark period of suffering to change their lives.

It all began with a selfish Pharaoh, or king of Egypt. At first, one Pharaoh had welcomed the Israelites into Egypt. But later another Pharaoh grew jealous of their loyalty to the one, true God. He also grew afraid of their great numbers and strength. He decided to control God's people by making them his slaves. Then he commanded that every one of their newborn sons be thrown into the river.

God's people were confused and crushed with sorrow. But God never left them. He made a plan to set His people free. He chose an Israelite called Moses to be His special helper. Moses' mother was able to save him from the Pharaoh's cruel command by putting her baby in a small basket woven of papyrus and hiding him among reeds of the river. It was the Pharaoh's daughter who discovered the child and took him home to the Egyptian palace. Moses grew up with the royal family, but he always knew he was an Israelite.

One day God spoke to Moses from a burning bush. He told Moses, "I hear the cries of My people. I know that they are suffering. Come now! I will send you to Pharaoh to lead My people, the Israelites, out of Egypt." At first Moses was afraid. He made many excuses. But finally he agreed to go because God promised him, "I will be with you and I will help you. Trust in Me."

Moses went to the Pharaoh as God commanded. "Let my people go!" he said. Moses warned the Pharaoh that he came in the name of God. The Pharaoh just laughed. He ignored Moses and treated the Israelite slaves even more harshly. God punished this cruel king by sending many plagues, or disasters, to his land. All the water in Egypt turned to blood. A huge number of frogs and bugs covered the crops and houses. Hailstorms swept across the land. Terrible illnesses hurt the Egyptian people. The country was plunged into darkness. Each time Pharaoh cried, "Stop this plague! I will let your people go!" But time and time again, the Pharaoh broke his promise. He had no intention of setting his slaves free.

Finally God sent the most terrible plague of all. He sent the Angel of Death to kill the first-born of every Egyptian home. The Israelites were spared this tragedy because they obeyed God's command that each family share a special meal after killing a lamb and sprinkling the lamb's blood on the doorposts of their houses. When the Angel of Death saw this sign, he passed over the house and it was safe. This was called the Passover meal. Therefore, only the Egyptians lost their first-born children. The Pharaoh was so full of grief, he finally gave in. He let the Israelite people go.

Moses led the People of God out of Egypt to safety. The escape was full of danger, for soon the Pharaoh changed his mind again and ordered his army to chase them. God protected His children by parting the Red Sea so they could run across it on foot. Then God closed the water, and it swallowed up the Pharaoh's men.

God protected the people in many more ways during their long journey to Canaan, the Promised Land. He gave them food and fresh water. He encouraged them when they were tired or losing hope. He invited Moses up to a mountain-top to receive Ten Commandments that would make His people holy and happy. Over and over again God lived up to His promise, or Covenant: "You will be My people, and I will be your God."

The God of Abraham and Moses is our God. There is only one, true God. He still speaks in our hearts today: "You will be My people, and I will be your God."

Words to Know:

Covenant   Moses   Pharaoh   Canaan

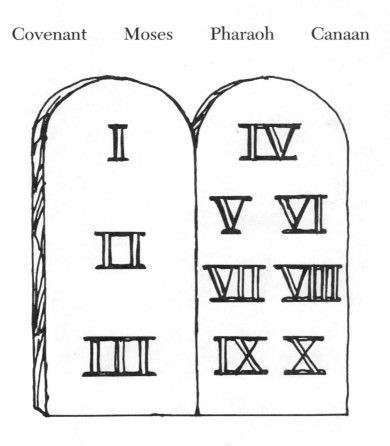

30

7 King David

Many years after the Israelites escaped from Egypt, they decided they wanted to have an earthly king like the other nations. God warned them against having a king, but since the Israelites really wanted one, He said yes. God told the holy prophet Samuel to anoint the new king by pouring oil over his head. This anointing was a sign of God's gift of power.

A man named Saul was chosen to be the king of Israel, but Saul turned out to be weak and disobedient to God. Therefore, God chose another king named David to rule over His people after Saul died. David was only a young shepherd boy, but he turned out to be a very great and wonderful king of Israel. He was a kind and strong leader, talented and clear-thinking in battle. He conquered Jerusalem and made it the city of his people. Best of all, King David really loved God. Sometimes he fell into sin, but he was always sorry and came back to God. He helped his people to lead good lives.

Two very special things about David teach us about friendship with God. One was his victory over the cruel champion Goliath. Goliath, who challenged the People of God, was over nine feet tall and carried a heavy metal sword. David, who stood up for the People of God, was small and had no sword. We would think that the boy David would not have a chance. And yet, David trusted God enough to fight Goliath, and he won. David showed his people that even when all hope seems lost, God is near us. God's strength and help are more powerful than anything else in this world.

A second thing that King David taught us was the importance of prayer, or talking with God. David used his beautiful voice and musical talents to make up songs for God. These Psalms, which are messages of praise and love, are still sung in the Church today, many centuries later. We sing them or read them at Mass because the words that David sang so long ago still express the same things we believe today: God is mighty and beautiful. His mercy is everlasting. We trust and love and adore Him. We are sorry for sin. We delight in the treasures of His creation. And we thank Him for sharing His life.

David was such a good king that God promised the Savior, the eternal King, would come into the world through his family. David, in fact, foreshadowed the Savior in many ways. Like Jesus, David was a good shepherd who took care of his flock. He was a wise and just king. He was willing to lay down his life for his people when he saved them from Goliath. He listened to the Father. David, the poet-king, was a hero in the course of God's plan to save mankind.

Words to Know:

king   prophet   David   Goliath   anoint

Read this Psalm from the Bible and listen carefully to the words.
Why do you think King David's poems are still so important today?
Can you make up a prayer of praise in words of your own?

The Lord is my shepherd;
   There is nothing I shall want.
   In green pastures He lays me down;
Beside restful waters He leads me;
   He refreshes my soul.
He guides me by paths of virtue
   for the sake of His name.
Even though I walk in the dark valley,
   I fear no harm, for You are at my side.

You prepare a table before me. . .
   You anoint my head with oil,
   my cup brims over.

Only goodness and kindness follow me
   all the days of my life;
And I shall dwell in the house of the Lord
   as long as I live!

(Psalm 23)

34

8   God's Laws of Love

After the children of God had safely escaped Egypt, they still had challenges to face. They had a long way to go before they reached the Promised Land. God had protected them on their way. He gave them quail meat, a bread-like food called manna, and fresh water. He gave them enough each day to satisfy their hunger and thirst.

God also wanted to nourish the souls of His children. He wanted to teach them how to love Him and be good to each other. One day, God called Moses, His prophet, to the top of Mount Sinai and gave him the rules of His Kingdom. We call these rules the Ten Commandments. God gave them to Moses written on stone tablets, but He wants them to be written on our hearts.

The first three Commandments told the people how to worship and respect God. The last seven told them how to be kind and fair to each other. The Commandments asked them to do some things and avoid others. God meant all ten of these to work together in our daily life. He also meant them to bring happiness and joy to His children's lives. He wanted to protect them from the sadness of sin.

Even though God gave the Ten Commandments to His people during the time of the Old Testament, they are meant for all God's people until the end of time.

When some people asked Jesus which of the Commandments was the greatest, He answered:

"You shall love the Lord your God with your whole heart,
and with your whole soul, and with your whole mind. This is
the greatest and the first Commandment. And the second is
like it, you shall love your neighbor as yourself."

Keeping God's Commandments is not always easy, but it is worth it. Some day we will see God face to face. If we have followed His Commandments on earth, He promises to share with us the joys of Heaven that last for ever.

Words to Know:

Commandment   Mount Sinai

Q. 18 *What are the Commandments of God?*
The Commandments of God are the moral laws which God gave to Moses on Mount Sinai in the Old Testament and which Jesus Christ perfected in the New Testament.

Q. 19 *Are we obliged to keep the Commandments of God?*
Yes, we are obliged to keep the Commandments of God because they are laid on us by Him Who is our Supreme Master, and they are indicated by our nature and by sound reason.

THE TEN COMMANDMENTS

1. You shall not have other gods before Me.
2. You shall not take the name of the Lord your God in vain.
3. Remember to keep holy the Lord's Day.
4. Honor your father and your mother.
5. You shall not kill.
6. You shall not commit adultery.
7. You shall not steal.
8. You shall not lie.
9. You shall not covet your neighbor's wife.
10. You shall not covet your neighbor's goods.

"If you love Me, keep my Commandments."
(John 14:15)

38

9 Loving God Most of All

Our God is so holy and magnificent that we can never love Him too much. He is our Creator and King. He is also a loving Father Who cares for us more than anyone else in the world can. We cannot see God, but He is with us all the time. Everything we have is a gift from Him. He gave us our life, our family, our beautiful world, and many other gifts.

Because God is perfect and can do all things, we give to Him something that we do not give to anyone else. We adore and worship Him. We pray to Him, believe in Him, hope in Him, and love Him. The angels also praise and adore God. They appeared to shepherds in Bethlehem when Jesus was born, singing, "Holy, Holy, Holy, Lord God of Hosts, Heaven and earth are filled with Your glory!"

God Himself told us in the First Commandment, "I am the Lord your God. You shall not have other gods before Me." In this Commandment, He asks us to know that He is the one, true God and to love Him above all things.

The "other gods" that God told us not to worship are everyday persons, places, or things that can lead us away from Him. Some examples might be money, pleasures, toys, or nice clothes. These things are good and we can enjoy them, but we must not let them take our attention away from God. The things of this earth will pass away, but God is for ever and He has destined us to live with Him for ever. Nothing on earth can compare with God and the treasures that He gives. That is why He comes first.

God does not want us to be superstitious. This would insult Our Lord instead of giving Him glory.

The Second Commandment is: "You shall not take the name of the Lord your God in vain." We are only to use the name of God to speak to Him or about Him in a reverent or loving way.

People in the Old Testament knew how great God is, so they were very careful when they spoke His name. When Jesus came to earth, He encouraged us to call on God's name often. He taught us a prayer that we still say together at every Mass. "Our Father, Who art in Heaven, hallowed be Thy name. . . ." Hallowed means holy. The name of God is holy and it has power. We know this because the apostles worked many miracles in Jesus' name. Jesus promised, "Whatever you ask in My name will be done."

The name of Jesus is just as powerful today. If you are lonely or afraid, call on Jesus' name. He will come to you. If you are confused or have a problem at home or at school, call on Jesus' name. He will help you. Jesus hears us every time we call. At Benediction, we praise Him for this by joyfully saying, "Blessed be God. Blessed be His holy name."

The Second Commandment also tells us to respect holy places and things. A church is a holy place. When we go into a church, we can show love for God by quietly listening to the priest and obeying our parents. We can look at the tabernacle or Jesus on the crucifix, and we can pray. We should genuflect and make the Sign of the Cross when we leave. God will bless us for these acts of love.

Whether we are in a church, a park, our home, or going somewhere in a car, we can always praise God by telling Him silently and quietly that we believe in Him, hope in Him, and love Him most of all.

Words to Know:

superstition   reverent   respect

A Song of Praise:

HOLY GOD WE PRAISE THY NAME

Holy God we praise Thy name!
    Lord of all, we bow before Thee!
All on earth Thy scepter 'claim.
    All in Heaven above adore Thee.
Infinite Thy vast domain,
    Everlasting is Thy reign!

Q. 20 *What are we told positively to do by the First Commandment, "I am the Lord your God; you shall not have other gods before Me"?*
The First Commandment, "I am the Lord your God; you shall not have other gods before Me" commands us to be religious, that is, to believe in God and to love Him, to adore Him and to serve Him as the one true God, the Creator and Lord of all things.

Q. 21 *What does the First Commandment prohibit?*
The First Commandment prohibits impiety, superstition, irreligious behavior; and, in addition, apostasy, heresy, voluntary doubt, and culpable ignorance of the truths of faith.

Q. 22 *What is forbidden by the Second Commandment?*

The Second Commandment forbids us to dishonor the name of God, that is, to take His name without respect; to blaspheme God or the most holy Virgin, the saints or holy things; and to swear oaths that are false, not necessary, or wrong in any way.

Q. 23 *What are we ordered to do by the Second Commandment?*

The Second Commandment orders us to maintain always a reverence for the name of God, and to fulfill the vows and promises to which we have bound ourselves.

"O Lord, our God, how glorious is Your name over all the earth!"

(Psalm 8:10)

10   The Lord's Day

When God created the world, He worked for six days and on the seventh He rested. God values the work we do, but He wants us to take one day of the week to rest too. He also wants us to use that day to join others in worship. In the Old Testament, God's people stopped working and gathered together for worship on the Sabbath, or Saturday. However, the early Christians rested and came together to rejoice on Sunday because Jesus, Our Lord and Savior, rose from the dead on Easter Sunday morning.

We still keep Sunday as a special day to celebrate the miracle of the Resurrection. God is very pleased when we do this because His Third Commandment to us is, "Remember to keep holy the Lord's Day."

The greatest gift that we can offer to God on His day is to go to Mass faithfully. At every Mass, we give ourselves to God and join ourselves with Christ's gift of Himself to the Father. The Father in turn gives us His own Son as "the Bread of Life", Who nourishes our souls. This makes Sunday not only a day of praise but also a day of blessings and joy.

Holy Days of Obligation like Christmas, All Saints' Day, the Feast of the Ascension, and the Feast of the Immaculate Conception are considered just as special as Sundays. They are days we mark as celebrations or feasts of special worship. God wants us to keep those days holy, too, by praying and going to Mass.

Sunday is not only a day of worship but a day of joy and family closeness. It is a day when we put work aside and take time to relax. We can do that by going on a picnic, playing games, talking and laughing, or enjoying a special dinner together. It is also a good day

44

to visit relatives or invite neighbors into our home. Just like the Risen Lord, Who spent Easter Sunday sharing peace and joy with His friends, we are meant to reach out and spread warmth and happiness to others. This is part of God's plan for our holiness.

Words to Know:

Holy Day of Obligation

Q. 24 *What are we ordered to do by the Third Commandment?*
The Third Commandment orders us to honor God on Sundays and Holy Days of Obligation by acts of external worship, and for Christians the most important of these is the Holy Mass.

Q. 25 *What is forbidden by the Third Commandment?*
The Third Commandment forbids us to do unnecessary "servile works" on Sundays and Holy Days of Obligation.

"This is the day the Lord has made. Let us be glad and rejoice in it."

(Psalm 118)

46

11   Obedience and Love

We bring happiness to our home when we live up to God's Fourth Commandment: "Honor your father and your mother."

God wants us to honor our parents because He brought us into the world through them. They gave us life. And once we were born, they gave us much more. Ever since we were little tiny babies, our parents have loved, protected, and guided us. God entrusted us especially to them for that reason. They work and make sacrifices for us. They care for us every day. They give us all we need, whether it is a good, hot dinner, new clothes as we grow, or surprises for our birthday.

Above all, they care for our souls. They want us to be good, so that we will be happy not only in this world but also for all eternity in Heaven. That is why they had us baptized and want us to receive the sacraments and learn about our faith.

When the Christ Child was growing up in Nazareth, He had many chances to love and obey His mother and foster father, Joseph. Joseph was a carpenter and Jesus helped him carry the wood and hammer the nails. He surely also helped His mother Mary. We can picture Jesus doing these things kindly and cheerfully. Even though He was God, He respected His parents enough to obey and listen to them.

We discover the secret of the Holy Family's happiness every time we obey and offer to help. Some days it is hard to obey our parents because we would really rather play outside or go somewhere with our friends. When this happens, just remember that making sacrifices of love makes us happiest of all in the end. Doing the right thing can be hard sometimes, but it will make us happy. Doing the

47

wrong thing leaves a feeling of sadness inside us. This is part of our human nature because God made us to love Him, and we can only be happy when we obey the Commandments.

God wants us to respect and obey, not only our parents, but others who have lawful authority to protect us. For example, if we are at school and our teacher asks us to put away our artwork, listen without talking, or help a classmate who is in trouble we obey, and then we please God.

In the Fourth Commandment God tells us to honor our father and mother who gave us life. In the Fifth Commandment, God asks us to respect all human life. "You shall not kill", He tells us.

The life of every person, no matter how poor or old or small, belongs to God and is precious. When you were inside your mother's womb and small enough to fit in the palm of a hand, God loved you and had a plan for your life. That is why the life of every baby inside of his mother is sacred and we respect it.

God wants us to respect the lives of people around us. In the Gospel, Jesus told the story of a man who was attacked by robbers when he was going down the road. They took his money and clothes and left him half dead. Three people passed the wounded man. The first two ignored him. The third one stopped to clean and bandage the man's wounds. Then he took the man to an inn and paid for his care and shelter. Jesus said that this Good Samaritan acted the way He wants us to act, especially toward the suffering and the poor. God will reward us if we show good will and a readiness to make sacrifices for others. He will bless us whenever we value, protect, or save the lives of others. Jesus said: "I tell you solemnly, as you did it to one of the least of these brothers of Mine, you did it to Me" (Matthew 25:40).

On the other hand, it saddens God when we say mean things in anger, or refuse to make up with a friend after a fight. He wants us to

48

be forgiving, loving, and generous. In our lifetime, He will give us many chances to be kind. We are kind when we help someone who is sick or handicapped. We are kind when we hug a little brother or sister after he or she has fallen down. We are kind when we pray for people we do not like.

God wants us to respect our own lives too. Our lives are a gift we must protect. When we try to eat the right foods to stay healthy or when we cross the street only when it is safe, we show God that we value His gift of life.

Words to Know:

obey   good will   honor

> **Q. 26** *What does the Fourth Commandment order us to do?*
> The Fourth Commandment orders us to love, respect, and obey our parents and whoever holds authority over us, that is, those who are our superiors.
>
> **Q. 27** *What does the Fifth Commandment forbid?*
> The Fifth Commandment forbids us to harm the life, either natural or spiritual, of our neighbor as well as of ourselves. It prohibits murder, suicide, fighting (out of anger), cursing, and giving scandal.

Q. 28 *What are we ordered to do by the Fifth Commandment?*
The Fifth Commandment orders us to be of good will toward all, including our enemies, and to make good any bodily or spiritual evil we do to our neighbor.

"I will never forget you. See, I have carved you on the palm of My hand."

(Isaiah 49:15—16)

12   Purity and Truth

Have you ever thought about how important your body is? You speak with your body. You run, walk, and stand up to help someone with your body. With your five senses of touch, taste, sight, smell, and hearing, you are able to enjoy and learn about the world, and bring your talents to it.

God gave you your voice, your eyes, your hands, and all of your body for many wonderful reasons. Your body is holy because on the day of your Baptism, the Holy Spirit came to live inside of it. In the Sixth and Ninth Commandments, God told us to respect our bodies and the bodies of other people. He wants us to keep our bodies pure and pleasing to Him. He wants us to be modest and to stay away from movies, books, and pictures that are not modest.

God also wants us to be faithful in our relationships with other people. For example, someday we may marry a person we love. God will expect us to be faithful to the love and promises we vow on that day. If we make ourselves strong to live up to that love, God will reward us richly.

The Seventh Commandment and the Tenth Commandment tell us to be fair with property. God wants us to be satisfied with what we have, not to covet what others have. We are also to respect other people's things. God told us, "You shall not steal." If someone takes a snack or a toy or money that belongs to someone else, he is breaking God's law. Cheating on tests, borrowing things and not returning them, or being dishonest in a store breaks the same law.

We can obey the Seventh and Tenth Commandments by being satisfied with the things we have, by taking care of them, and by sharing them. It pleases God when we give or share a snack, a toy, or money that belongs to us.

52

God also wants us to take special care of other people's things. If we borrow a book from the library, we should take good care of it and return it on time. If we accidentally break something that belongs to someone else, God wants us to make up for it, either by paying for it or replacing it. This is called justice or fairness.

If four children are playing ball on the front lawn and by mistake their ball smashes a neighbor's window, they have some choices. They can run away and pretend it did not happen. They can lie and say that someone else broke the window. They can keep playing ball and not worry about it. Or they can go to the neighbor, tell him what really happened, then help pay for the damage. Which choice do you think obeys the Seventh and Tenth Commandments?

The Eighth Commandment tells us to be honest: "You shall not bear false witness against your neighbor" (tell a lie). This means that we should always speak the truth. God loves the truth. When Jesus was on earth He spoke the truth in all things, even when it did not make Him popular. He wants us to do the same.

Sometimes we are afraid to tell the truth or we want to blame someone else for something we did. But God asks that we be honest with ourselves and others. If we are truthful and keep our promises, we will be like Jesus Who is the Truth.

Many holy people have even died for the truth. St. Thomas More is one example. He was a special friend and helper of King Henry the Eighth in England during the sixteenth century. One day the king decided to disobey God and make himself head of the Church. He asked Thomas More to agree with him. But Thomas refused because this was not right. The king's judges tried to force Thomas to lie. When they could not succeed, they put him to death. Thomas told the English people, "I die the king's good servant, but God's first." Thomas More had integrity, which means he was true to himself and to God. His honesty helped him get to Heaven.

Can you think of any other saints or holy people who have suffered to witness to the truth?

Words to Know:

purity   honesty   truth   covet
bear false witness   vow

Q. 29 *What are we forbidden by the Eighth Commandment?*
The Eighth Commandment prohibits all falsehood and unjust damage regarding another person's reputation. This includes false witness, lies, flattery, unfounded suspicion, and rash judgment.

Q. 30 *What does the Eighth Commandment order?*
The Eighth Commandment orders us to speak the truth carefully and to interpret in the best possible way the actions of our neighbor.

Q. 31 *To what is a person obliged who has damaged his neighbor in his good name by accusing him falsely or speaking wickedly of him?*
He who has damaged his neighbor in his good name by false accusation or wicked talk about him, must repair the damage he has done, so far as he is able.

Q. 32 *What does the Sixth Commandment forbid?*
The Sixth Commandment forbids impurity of any kind; this means immoral words, books, pictures, and shows.

Q. 33 *What does the Ninth Commandment forbid?*
The Ninth Commandment forbids deliberate impure thoughts and desires.

Q. 34 *What is forbidden by the Seventh Commandment?*
The Seventh Commandment forbids damaging our neighbor in his property. This includes thefts and damaging actions. It also forbids giving assistance to those who commit such damages.

Q. 35 *What does the Seventh Commandment order us to do?*
The Seventh Commandment orders us to make restitution of property belonging to others, to repair damages that we cause, and to honor our debts.

"Blessed are the pure of heart, for they shall see God."

(Matthew 5:8)

Q. 36 *Does he who fails to make restitution of property or repair damage, although he is able to do so, obtain pardon?*
He who, although able, does not make restitution or repair damage, will not obtain pardon, even though by his words he declares himself repentant.

Q. 37 *What does the Tenth Commandment forbid?*
The Tenth Commandment forbids the unbridled desire for riches, without regard for the rights and welfare of our neighbors.

Q. 38 *What does the Tenth Commandment order us to do?*
The Tenth Commandment orders us to be just and moderate in the desire to improve our own condition of life, and to suffer with patience the hardships and other sufferings permitted by the Lord for our merit, because "we must undergo many trials if we are to enter into the reign of God" (Acts 14:22).

"He who lies is a fool, but the tongue of a just man is as choice silver."

(Proverbs 10:18—20)

13   God's Tender Mercy

Jesus told many stories to show us how deep God's love is. God's love follows us wherever we go. Even when we commit sins, God does not stop loving us. He waits and watches for us to return. The moment we say we are sorry, He welcomes us back with open arms. No sin on earth will ever be greater than His mercy and love.

Jesus told the story about a shepherd who loved his sheep. The shepherd gave his flock fresh water and food. He protected it from wolves. He knew each lamb by name and was willing to lay down his life for them in danger. One day a lamb got lost and the shepherd did not rest until he found it. When the lamb came back, the shepherd said, "Rejoice with me, because I have found my lost sheep." Then Jesus told us He was the Good Shepherd and we were His sheep. He compared the story to His love for us: "In the same way, there is great joy in Heaven whenever anyone is sorry for his sins."

Jesus did more than tell stories about forgiveness. He forgave many sinners. Some of the sinners were among His own friends. Peter the apostle denied Jesus three times on the night He was betrayed. After Peter realized what he had done and wept with sorrow, Jesus forgave him completely.

Jesus' love and mercy gave hope to people with very bad sins. It invited them to be good. Mary Magdalen was a great sinner, but she believed in Jesus and the Good News of God's love. One night she came up to Jesus, poured precious oil on His feet, and wept for forgiveness. That was all Mary had to do. Jesus told everyone, "This woman's sins are forgiven because she has loved much."

Only God can forgive sins. But on the first Easter Sunday night, Jesus gave His apostles the power to forgive sins in His name. This

was a gift of grace to the world. Jesus breathed on the apostles and said, "Peace be with you. Receive the Holy Spirit; if you forgive men's sins, they are forgiven."

The apostles were the early priests of the Church. Our priests today carry the same power to forgive sins. They do this through the sacrament of Penance. This sacrament frees our souls of any mortal sins, which are very serious and rob us of grace. It also frees us of less serious, venial sins. When we go to a priest for this sacrament, we can be sure that Christ Himself is present, and He washes away all our sins. He will never turn us away when we are truly sorry for our sins, but He will only hold us closer to His Heart.

Remember, Jesus was crucified on a Cross between two thieves. The thief on Jesus' left had no sorrow for his crimes. But the thief on Jesus' right cried out that he was sorry. Jesus forgave him and said to him, "This very day you will be with Me in Paradise" (Luke 23:43).

Words to Know:

mortal sin   venial sin   grace   forgiveness

Q. 39 *What is actual sin?*
Actual sin is a sin which is committed voluntarily by one who has the use of reason.

Q. 40 *In how many ways is actual sin committed?*
Actual sin is committed in four ways, in *thoughts*, in *words*, in *deeds*, and in *omissions*.

Q. 41 *How many kinds of actual sin are there?*
Actual sin is of two kinds: *mortal* and *venial*.

Q. 42 *What is mortal sin?*
Mortal sin is a serious act of disobedience against the law of God.

Q. 43 *What is venial sin?*
Venial sin is a little act of disobedience against the law of God.

Q. 44 *Are all sins equal?*
Sins are not all equal. And just as some venial sins are less light than others, so some mortal sins are more serious and harmful than others.

Q. 45 *What is Confession?*
Confession is the sacrament instituted by Jesus Christ to forgive the sins committed after Baptism.

Q. 46 *When was the sacrament of Confession instituted by Jesus Christ?*
The sacrament of Confession was instituted by Jesus Christ when he said to the apostles and in them to their successors: "Receive the Holy Spirit: if you forgive men's sins, they are forgiven them; if you hold them bound, they are held bound" (John 20:22—23).

14 Meeting Jesus In Confession

If you know you have hurt someone you love, what should you do? The best thing to do is to go to that person and say you are sorry. It is not enough just to think about how sorry you are. A good friendship calls for more. A true friend will go to the person he has hurt, say he is sorry, and make up and be friends again.

In the sacrament of Penance, that is what we do with Jesus. We go to Him, tell Him we are sorry, resolve not to sin again, accept His forgiveness, and keep our friendship with Him alive and strong.

To prepare ourselves for this Sacrament, there are certain things we must do. First we ask God the Holy Spirit, Who lives inside us, to help us remember our sins. We think about what we have done wrong and how many times we have done it.

Next, we think about how our sins offend Jesus and we are sorry for them. We make up our minds not to commit the same sins again, and we say an Act of Contrition. Contrition means sorrow. An Act of Contrition is a prayer telling God we are sorry and we hate our sins. In the Act of Contrition we say we hate sin because we know it can keep us from Heaven, but much more importantly, because it offends God. We tell God that He is all good and deserving of all our love. We ask for His grace to do better in the future.

After our silent Act of Contrition, it is time to receive the sacrament. We go into the confessional or reconciliation room where the priest welcomes us. Together we make the Sign of the Cross. The priest may read to us from the Bible. Usually there are words about God's mercy and love.

We tell the priest how long it has been since our last confession, then we confess our sins since that time. After we are all finished, the priest talks to us about what we have told him. Then he gives us a penance, which can be some prayers or action that helps to make up for the wrong we have done to God and to others. (We will do the penance after our confession is over.) Then we say the Act of Contrition out loud.

Before we leave the confessional, the priest will absolve us. This means that he uses his Christ-given power to forgive all our sins. When we hear the words of absolution, we know that Jesus Himself is forgiving us through the priest. He says, "I absolve you from your sins in the name of the Father, and of the Son, and of the Holy Spirit." We accept the absolution by answering, "Amen." This is a beautiful moment, because God has completely forgiven us. He is giving us a fresh start.

Every time we receive the sacrament of Penance, Jesus is with us, healing our hearts. We always confess our sins privately to a priest, usually in the confessional. Sometimes, at a communal Penance service, all the people in the church prepare together for Confession and then confess and receive absolution individually. In cases of necessity where to hear individual confessions of large numbers of people is impossible, a priest may give general absolution to all the people. But those people then have to make a private, individual confession as soon as they are able.

Jesus waits for us in this sacrament because He has so much grace to give us. Let us try to go to Him often.

Words to Know:

examination of conscience   penance
sorrow for sins   contrition
sacrament of Penance

63

ACT OF CONTRITION

Oh my God, I am heartily sorry for having offended You. I detest all my sins because of Your just punishments, but most of all because they offend You, my God, Who are all-good and deserving of all my love. I firmly resolve, with the help of Your grace, to confess my sins, to do penance, and to amend my life. *Amen*.

THE WORDS OF ABSOLUTION

God, the Father of mercies, through the death and Resurrection of His Son, has reconciled the world to Himself and sent the Holy Spirit among us for the forgiveness of sins; through the ministry of the Church, may God give you pardon and peace, and I absolve you from your sins in the name of the Father, and of the Son, and of the Holy Spirit.

Q. 47 *How many things are required to make a good confession?*

To make a good confession five things are required: 1) examination of conscience; 2) sorrow for sins; 3) the intention of not committing sin again; 4) the accusation of our sin; 5) satisfaction or penance.

Q. 48 *How is the examination of conscience done?*

The examination of conscience is done by recalling to mind the sins we have committed in thoughts, words, and omissions against the Commandments of God, beginning from our last good confession.

Q. 49 *What is sorrow?*

Sorrow or repentance is displeasure and hatred for the sins we have committed, which bring us to form the intention of not sinning again.

66

15 The Christ Child Is Born

How would you feel if you and your family sat for a long time in a cold, dark room with no light? That is how the people of Israel might sometimes have felt during their long wait for the Messiah. They waited in darkness for two thousand years. At last God kept His promise. He sent the world a Savior Who shattered the darkness with a great light.

God did not send a rich king or strong warrior to be the Light of the World. He sent a little child. This child was His own Son, Jesus. Jesus is God, but He was born into the world as a man like us. God the Father invited Mary to be a part of this special plan to save His people. Jesus came to the world because Mary answered "yes".

Mary was a young woman of Nazareth. She was in her simple, village home one day when the angel Gabriel appeared before her to bring God's message:

> "Hail, full of grace, the Lord is with you! Blessed are you among women! You will bear a son and call His name Jesus, for He shall save His people from their sins. The Holy Spirit will come upon you and the power of the Most High will overshadow you, and so the holy Child to be born shall be called the Son of God."

Mary knew if she said "yes" it might mean great sorrows as well as great joys. But she wanted to do whatever God asked. She bowed her head and told the angel: "Behold the handmaid of the Lord, let it be done to me according to your word." Mary's quiet "yes" was still a secret to God's people, but it was the beginning of His loving plan to rescue them.

An ordinary girl might have been afraid. But Mary was special. God prepared her to be the mother of the Savior even before she was born. He had given her a gift which we call Mary's Immaculate Conception. This means that Mary was created free from original sin. From the moment she was conceived in her mother's womb, her soul was filled with sanctifying grace. Mary did not need to be baptized because she always had God's life in her soul. This is why she was worthy to be the mother of Jesus. God also chose a good man named Joseph to marry her and be the foster father of Jesus.

On the night of Jesus' birth, Mary and Joseph walked from inn to inn looking for shelter. They were in Bethlehem at the Roman governor's request that all people return to their hometowns. The little town of Bethlehem was full. Every innkeeper told Joseph, "Sorry, there is no room for you in this inn."

At last, Joseph found a stable under the stars. Animals were sheltered beneath its roof. Jesus was born that night among the gentle oxen, donkeys, and lambs. Mary wrapped Him tenderly in soft cloth and laid Him in a manger. The Son of God spent His first earthly hours on a humble bed of straw.

An angel appeared to shepherds on the hillsides near Bethlehem and proclaimed, "Behold, I bring you Good News of great joy! Today, in the town of David, has been born to you a Savior, Who is Christ the Lord. You will find Him lying in a manger." Full of wonder, the shepherds ran to be the first to adore Him. Later three wise men followed a great star to find the Child. They brought Him precious gifts for a King. We can bring the Christ Child our hearts.

"Glory to God in the highest, and on earth peace to men of good will."

(Luke 2:14)

Words to Know:

Bethlehem   humble
foster father   manger   stable

Q. 50 *Did Jesus Christ always exist?*
As God, Jesus Christ has always existed; as man, He began to exist from the moment of the Incarnation.

Q. 51 *From whom was Jesus Christ born?*
Jesus Christ was born of Mary ever-virgin, who therefore is called and is truly the Mother of God.

Q. 52 *But was not St. Joseph the father of Jesus Christ?*
St. Joseph was not the *true* father of Jesus Christ; as the spouse of Mary and the guardian of Jesus, he was *believed* to be His true father, although actually he was not.

Q. 53 *Where was Jesus Christ born?*
Jesus Christ was born at Bethlehem, in a stable, and He was placed in a manger.

Q. 54 *Why did Jesus Christ wish to be poor?*
Jesus Christ wished to be poor in order to teach us to be humble and not to place our happiness in the riches, the honors, and the pleasures of this world.

Christmas is Jesus' birthday. Every year we sing carols to celebrate. This carol was written over a hundred years ago:

WE THREE KINGS OF ORIENT ARE

We three kings of Orient are;
Bearing gifts we traverse afar,
Field and fountain, moor and mountain,
Following yonder star.

O star of wonder, star of night,
Star with royal beauty bright,
Westward leading, still proceeding,
Guide us to thy perfect light.

Born a King on Bethlehem's plain,
Gold I bring, to crown Him again,
King for ever, ceasing never,
Over us all to reign.

16   Jesus Grows in Age and Wisdom

As a boy growing up in Nazareth, Jesus led an ordinary life. He ate, slept, laughed, played, worked, and studied. Even though He was God, He was truly a human and He grew up and learned things just as we do. Since Jesus was Jewish, He learned all the Jewish customs and traditions of His time.

Joseph, a skilled carpenter, probably taught Jesus how to make fine things from wood. As a tiny boy, Jesus could only watch and pick up the wood chips as they fell. The neighbors of the Holy Family must have loved Jesus very much, but they had no idea that He was God's own Son. Only Mary and Joseph knew that. It was still hidden from the rest of the world. That is why we call the first thirty years of Jesus' time on earth His "hidden life".

Even though Jesus was living a "hidden" life, none of it was hidden from God the Father. God watched every moment of it. God sees every moment of *our* hidden lives too. He sees all the times we sacrifice something we would rather do to obey our parents. For example, you might want to call a friend, but your mother needs you to set the table. Or you might want to finish a book, but your father needs you to help him rake the lawn. When we offer up our little disappointments or boredom and obey our parents with love, God sees it all. He blesses us for acting as Jesus did when He was growing up.

When the time came, Jesus left His quiet life in Nazareth. He put away the tools of a carpenter and started working with the minds and hearts of living people.

72

God sent a prophet to prepare the way for Jesus. This prophet told people in a loud, clear voice, "Get ready! The Promised One is coming! Be sorry for your sins." This holy man was named John the Baptist. He baptized all the people who listened and were sorry for their sins.

One day Jesus Himself came to John to be baptized in the waters of the Jordan River. As Jesus came out of the water, God gave a wonderful sign. The Holy Spirit came down upon Him in the form of a dove, and the voice of His Father called from Heaven: "This is My Beloved Son with Whom I am well pleased." Now Jesus was ready to begin His public life in His mission as the Savior of the world.

At your own Baptism, the Holy Spirit came upon you too. He came inside your soul and filled it with grace. On that happy day, God silently told you, "You are My beloved child, and I love you." Just as with Jesus, our Baptism has prepared us for a mission. Our mission on earth is to love God with all our hearts and to love each other.

Words to Know:

John the Baptist

"And Jesus grew in wisdom, age, and grace before God and men."

(Luke 2:52)

74

17   Signs and Wonders

When He was about thirty years old, Jesus the Savior began making His presence clear to the people of God. He started preaching the Good News of the Kingdom of God in the area called Galilee. Crowds came from all over to hear Him speak. They were fascinated because Jesus was telling them things they had never heard before. He told them, "I am the Way, the Truth, and the Life."

Jesus performed many miracles to prove He was the Savior and the Son of God. Once a bride and groom in Cana ran out of wine at their wedding feast. Jesus solved their problem by changing the water in six stone jars into good wine.

Another time, Jesus fed a crowd of five thousand on five loaves of bread and two fish! People had crowded the hillsides all day to hear Him preach, and Jesus knew they were hungry. The apostles warned Him there was not enough food. Jesus blessed the handful of loaves and fishes and suddenly there was enough food for everyone. All five thousand people were amazed to get a delicious dinner in the hills that day.

Most of the time, Jesus performed miracles to heal the suffering. At His word or touch, the blind saw light, the lame walked, and the sick got well. All of this gave people great faith in Jesus.

Once a Roman soldier trusted in Jesus' power so much that he asked Jesus to heal his sick servant. When Jesus said, "I will go to heal him", the soldier said, "Lord, I am not worthy that You should come under my roof. Only say the word, and I know my servant will be healed." Jesus marveled at this man's trust and belief. He said, "Go your way. Because you have believed, your servant is cured." Later the Roman soldier learned that his servant had been cured at that very instant.

The Roman centurion's trust in Jesus' power to heal is remembered every time we go to Holy Mass. Right before Holy Communion we tell Jesus, "Lord, I am not worthy to receive You, but only say the word and I shall be healed."

Jesus' power to perform miracles was even stronger than death. He brought back to life a man named Lazarus who had been buried for four days. All hope seemed lost, but Jesus promised Lazarus' good sisters, "Your brother will rise." Then He ordered the stone to be rolled back from the tomb, and He called to Lazarus. Lazarus arose, alive and well, and all the people rejoiced in amazement.

"When the people, therefore, had seen the sign which Jesus had worked, they said, 'This is indeed the Prophet Who is come into the world.'"

(John 6:14)

Jesus came to heal people's souls. He taught them to love God the Father, to stop sinning, and to be holy. He gave them parables, or stories, that explained the Kingdom of God. One parable was about a mustard seed. A mustard seed is very tiny, but when planted in the ground it grows to be a huge tree. Jesus compared the mustard seed to His own Kingdom. It had small beginnings, but would cover the whole world.

He told another parable about a farmer sowing seeds. Some of the seeds fell on good ground and they yielded a rich harvest. Other seeds fell on rocks and thorns and they yielded nothing. Jesus said the seeds were like the Word of God falling on the ears of good men and bad men. If it falls on the good soil of a faithful heart, it yields many good things. If it falls on the poor soil of a stubborn heart, it can yield nothing at all.

Jesus found both friends and enemies on earth. His friends were the apostles and disciples who followed Him. His enemies were the ones who doubted and made fun of Him. These enemies could not understand a Savior Who ate with sinners and Who loved the poor. Many of the Jewish leaders, such as the Pharisees, were jealous of Jesus. They hated Him because He pointed out their faults. They were too proud to follow Jesus' teachings of love because it would mean changing their lives. They did not have the courage to become humble, forgiving, and loving like Jesus.

Q. 55 *What is the Son of God made man called?*
The Son of God made man is called Jesus Christ.

Q. 56 *Who is Jesus Christ?*
Jesus Christ is the Second Person of the Most Holy Trinity, that is, the Son of God made man.

Q. 57 *Is Jesus Christ God and man?*
Yes, Jesus Christ is true God and true man.

Words to Know:

miracle   parable

18 The Last Supper, Our First Mass

The night before Jesus died, He and the apostles gathered to celebrate the feast of Passover. This Jewish feast was a holy dinner held once a year. It honored the sacred memory of the time when God saved Moses and His Chosen People from slavery in Egypt.

This Passover night that Jesus and His apostles gathered, God was about to save His people again. This time He would save them from the darkness of sin and death. He would unlock the gates of Heaven and make it possible for them to live with Him in joy for ever.

Jesus, Our Savior, was about to pay a great price to win this grace. He was about to lay down His own life so that we could go to Heaven. Jesus knew His death was very near. Sitting at the Passover table that night, Jesus felt tender sadness at the thought of leaving His friends. He wanted them to be strong and holy when He was gone.

> "Little children, yet a little while I am with you. . . . A new Commandment I give you, that you love one another, that as I have loved you, you also love one another. By this will all men know that you are My disciples, if you have love for one another."
>
> (John 13:33–35)

80

First Jesus gave them a lesson in holiness. He knelt down to wash their feet. Peter told Him, "Master, You will never wash my feet." However, Jesus told Peter that friends love and serve one another without shame. He told the Twelve Apostles, "If I, the Lord and Master, have washed your feet, you also ought to wash the feet of one another. For I have given you an example; that as I have done to you, so you also should do."

Later, while they were eating, a very important moment came. Jesus took bread, blessed and broke it, and gave it to His disciples saying, "This is My Body, which will be given up for you."

Then He took a cup of wine. He gave thanks and gave it to them saying, "This is the Cup of My Blood, the Blood of the new and everlasting Covenant. It will be shed for you, and for all, so that sins may be forgiven."

When Jesus spoke those words, the bread and wine were changed into His Body and Blood. It still looked and tasted like ordinary food, but it was Jesus. When the apostles ate it, Jesus came into their souls. They were the first ones ever to receive Holy Communion.

Jesus told the apostles, "Do this in remembrance of Me." With these words, Jesus gave the apostles the power to do the same from that night on.

The Last Supper was actually the first Mass. It took place on a Thursday, the night before Jesus died. Every year on Holy Thursday we especially remember the first Mass and Jesus' gift of the Holy Eucharist and of the priesthood.

Holy Communion was not meant just for the apostles. It was meant for all of Jesus' followers until the end of time. At every Holy Mass the priest says the same words over bread and wine, and they become the Body and Blood of Jesus. We call this the sacrament of the Holy Eucharist. Whenever we receive it, Jesus comes into our hearts, alive and full of love.

Words to Know:

Last Supper   Holy Thursday   remembrance

"I am the Bread of Life. He who comes to Me shall not hunger, and he who believes in Me shall never thirst."

(John 6:35)

19　Jesus Gives His Life for Us

After the Last Supper, Jesus went out to pray in the Garden of Olives. He asked His disciples to stay awake with Him for a little while, but they fell asleep. Jesus was alone in His agony.

Jesus saw all of our sins that night and it saddened Him. He thought of all the suffering He would accept to make up for them. Remember, Jesus was both God and man. As a man, He felt deep emotions. That night He felt sadness and fear. He asked God the Father, "If it is possible, take this suffering away from Me." But then He told Him, "Your will, not Mine, be done." God the Father sent an angel to comfort Him.

Later in the night, soldiers came to arrest Jesus. These soldiers were cruel, but Jesus was gentle and went with them. He knew He was about to fulfill His Father's plan for our salvation. Jesus bravely went before the high priest and Jewish leaders. He was silent when they accused Him and wanted Him to be put to death.

By law, the Jewish leaders could not touch Jesus until they had the permission of Pontius Pilate, the Roman governor of Judea. He had the power to set Jesus free. He knew Jesus was innocent. But Pilate was too afraid of not being popular. When an angry crowd kept yelling out, "Crucify Him!" Pilate gave up. He did not protect Jesus. He sentenced Him to death as His enemies wanted.

The soldiers grabbed Jesus and treated Him like a criminal. They beat Him with whips. They pushed a crown of sharp thorns on His head. They made fun of Him by saying in disrespectful voices, "Hail, King of the Jews."

84

Now Jesus was very weak, but the soldiers hurt Him even more. They made Him carry a heavy Cross. They gave Him no rest or water. Jesus fell down three times, but they made Him go on. When Jesus reached the top of Mount Calvary, they nailed His hands and feet to the wood, raised the Cross, and left Him to die in pain.

Even in the midst of great suffering, Jesus was full of love. He asked His Father to forgive the cruel soldiers. He gave hope and forgiveness to a thief hanging by His side. He told His mother Mary to be the mother of His beloved apostle John, and of the whole world.

"Let not your heart be troubled. . . . I go to prepare a place for you. And if I go and prepare a place for you, I am coming again, and I will take you to Myself; that where I am, there also you may be."

(John 14:1–3)

Some of the people laughed at Jesus and said, "He heals others, but He cannot save Himself!" Jesus was God, and He had full power to escape the pain of the Cross. But He stayed on the Cross. He freely chose to suffer and die because He loved us so much. He wanted to make up for our sins. He wanted to redeem us so we could go to Heaven.

Jesus' sacrifice was so complete and so perfect that it conquered death for ever. It healed the wounds of Adam's sin. It restored full friendship between man and God.

Jesus' great victory taught us the value of sacrifice. His Passion and death saved the world. When we offer up things out of love, we are part of Jesus' great Sacrifice. We make up for our sins and the sins of others. In some way we help Him in saving the world. Small acts of self-denial can be as simple as giving up a piece of candy we want to keep or helping our mother when we are tired. These acts of love become part of Jesus' Sacrifice and help bring grace into the world.

Words to Know:

Calvary   sacrifice   Passion   redeem

Q. 58 *Why did the Son of God become man?*
The Son of God became man to save us, that is, to redeem us from sin and to regain Heaven for us.

Q. 59 *What did Jesus Christ do to save us?*
To save us, Jesus Christ made satisfaction for our sins by suffering and sacrificing Himself on the Cross, and He taught us how to live according to God.

Q. 60 *Did Jesus Christ die as God or as man?*
Jesus Christ died as man, because as God He could neither suffer nor die.

Q. 61 *What is a sacrifice?*
Sacrifice is the public offering to God of a thing which is destroyed to profess that God is the Creator and Supreme Master to Whom everything belongs.

The next time you go to Mass, find the Stations of the Cross in your church. Look at all fourteen images. Remember that Jesus loved you so much He suffered and died for you. You must be very precious to Him. Tell Him that you will love Him for ever.

STATIONS OF THE CROSS

1. Jesus is condemned to death.
2. Jesus carries His Cross.
3. Jesus falls the first time.
4. Jesus meets His Mother.
5. Jesus is helped by Simon.
6. Veronica wipes the face of Jesus.
7. Jesus falls a second time.
8. Jesus speaks to the women.
9. Jesus falls a third time.
10. Jesus is stripped of His clothes.
11. Jesus is nailed to the Cross.
12. Jesus dies on the Cross.
13. Jesus is taken down from the Cross.
14. Jesus is placed in the tomb.

"Greater love has no man than this, that a man lay down his life for his friends."

(John 15:13)

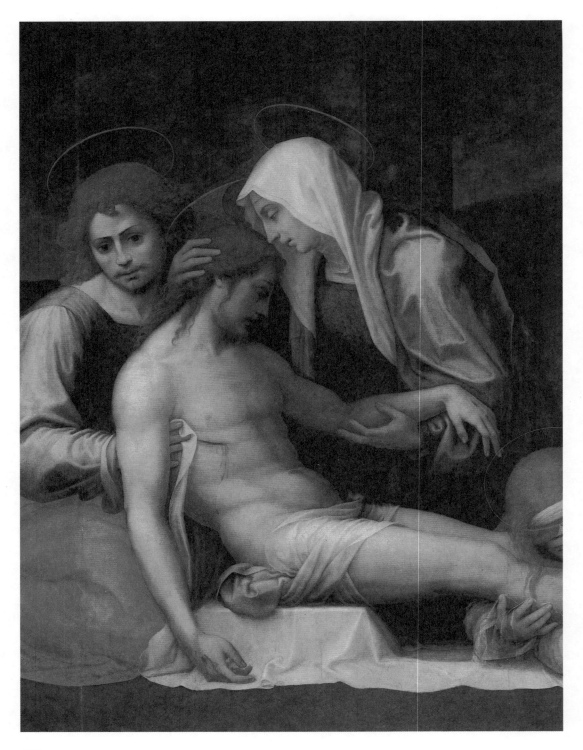

88

20 Offering Gifts of Love

All through the ages, God's children have offered sacrifices to Him as a sign of their worship and love. During the Old Testament days, before Jesus came to earth, the people of God offered up many things that were dear to them. In this way they told God that they loved His gifts, but they loved Him even more.

Whenever a person offered up something in sacrifice, he burned or destroyed it. This showed that he was giving it completely back to God. Farmers thanked God for their crops by sacrificing the first fruits of their harvest. It was a way of saying, "We believe that these gifts are from You. Thank You. Please keep blessing us."

So men made a present to the Heavenly Father of the very things that nourished them and kept them alive. Healthful grains like barley, wheat, and oats were baked into unleavened bread and cakes. Grapes were pressed into wine. Then the good grain and wine were given to God as gifts.

People of the Old Testament also offered up the bloody sacrifice of animals. They used cows, sheep, and doves. During an animal sacrifice, the priest placed the victim on an altar and put his hands on it. Then he killed the animal, shed its blood, and burned it.

Holy men of the Old Testament were generous in these sacrifices. Abel, who was a shepherd, offered up his best lamb. The first thing Noah did after the rains stopped was to build a stone altar and sacrifice some animals from the ark. Abraham was even willing to obey God's request that he sacrifice his own beloved son, Isaac. God was only testing Abraham's trust and love. He rewarded Abraham by stopping him and showing him a ram he could sacrifice instead.

In time, God had Moses appoint a few men to offer up gifts for all the people. These men were called priests. The people joined the priests in praying to God. Some of these prayers were cries for help or sorrow for sin. Others were gifts of praise or thanks.

Every Old Testament sacrifice had one great goal in common. Man deeply longed to make up for Adam's sin. He wanted to build a bridge back to God.

When Jesus came into the world, people were still trying to build that bridge. Families went to the Temple in Jerusalem to offer up lambs, doves, and food. God was pleased with these sacrifices. But He wanted to give His people a far greater gift to offer. He wanted to give them one gift that would unite them with Him to the end of time. And He wanted to give them a perfect gift.

When Jesus, His beloved Son, shed His blood and died on the Cross, He gave us that perfect gift. The Sacrifice of Himself was so perfect and true that it was the best gift ever given to God. It was so powerful that it washed away Adam's sin and redeemed the whole human race. It opened the Father's heart and the gates of Heaven.

Jesus knew that men and women in all of history would want to offer gifts to God too. So He made it possible for the perfect gift of His Body and Blood to be offered continually. On the night before He died, Jesus gave His apostles the power to change bread and wine into His Body and Blood. This act was the Sacrifice of the Mass.

Today all over the world the Sacrifice of the Mass continues in the same way. Listen to the words of the priest. "Take this, all of you, and eat it: this is My Body. . . . Take this, all of you, and drink from it: this is the Cup of My Blood. . . ." Every time we go to Holy Mass, we offer up Christ Himself to the Father. It is the very same Sacrifice as the one on Calvary.

On the Cross Jesus offered Himself, shedding His Blood for our redemption. Through the ministry of the priest Jesus is offered on the altar again without shedding His Blood. At Mass we not only

90

remember Jesus' Sacrifice of Himself to the Father, we continue it. Each time, Jesus brings His Sacrifice before us in a real but sacramental way. He is the Lamb of God being offered continually to save our world. Together with the priest we offer Him to the Father. This is the most pleasing and powerful gift we can ever give God. It is our most wonderful offering. It unites us with Him and fills our world with His life and love.

Words to Know:

Mass   Temple

Q. 62 *What is the Holy Mass?*
The Holy Mass is the Sacrifice of the Body and Blood of Jesus Christ, which is offered on the altar by the priest of God, under the appearances of bread and wine, in memory of the Sacrifice of the Cross and in *renewal* of the Sacrifice of the Cross.

Q. 63 *Is the Sacrifice of the Mass the same sacrifice as the Cross?*
The Sacrifice of the Mass is the very Sacrifice of the Cross; the only difference is in the manner of performing it.

21   The Holy Mass

Jesus' Sacrifice on the Cross healed a great wound. It reunited man and God in full friendship for the first time since the disobedience of Adam and Eve. This Sacrifice paid the price of our sins. It won back our glorious right to Heaven. It was the most perfect gift a man ever gave to God. Jesus became a man for this very purpose. The gift of His life was so powerful that He wants us to continue offering it to the Father until the end of time.

At the Last Supper, Jesus gave us a way to do that. He passed on to the apostles and all priests His power to bless and change the bread and wine. Now at every Mass this miracle happens. The priest turns the bread and wine into Christ's own Body and Blood. Then the priest lifts up the Host and Cup of wine and offers them to the Father. Christ, the Lamb of God, is sacrificed on the altar at Mass just as He was on Calvary. It is in a different way, but it is the very same Sacrifice.

We go to Mass every Sunday, and other days as well, to offer this gift to the Father. We also offer up our hearts and lives to Him. We offer all our joys and sufferings for His glory. We worship and adore Him. Sometimes we sing joyous songs of praise that voice our love.

At the beginning of the Mass, we make the Sign of the Cross. The priest asks us to call to mind our sins, and to ask for God's forgiveness. All together we say, "Lord have mercy, Christ have mercy." We thank God for His goodness in another prayer which begins "Glory to God. . . ."

Next we listen to readings from the Bible. On Sundays the first reading is usually taken from the Old Testament, the second from an Epistle, or letter, that one of the apostles wrote after Jesus returned to Heaven. These readings are messages of faith, hope, and love. They give us things to think about in our everyday lives.

After that, the priest reads to us from the Gospel. We stand during the Gospel reading because we are hearing Jesus' own words to us. For example, we might hear Jesus' parable, or story, of the Good Shepherd. At another Mass we may hear about one of Jesus' wonderful miracles. Every Sunday the Gospel gives us another message of love and hope. Remember, "Gospel" means Good News. The Good News of Christ's miracles, parables, and teachings is meant for us today, just as it was for His friends on earth two thousand years ago. The priest explains the Gospel message in a short talk called a homily. During the Gospel reading and the homily, it is very important to listen carefully.

After the homily, we stand with the priest to say the Creed. Creed means belief. Our Creed is a prayer that professes our faith. We say out loud that we believe in God the Father, the Creator of all things. We believe He sent His Son Jesus to save us from our sins. We believe God the Holy Spirit is alive among us. We say the Creed together at Mass because our faith is what binds us together as a Church.

Jesus comes into our hearts and lives at Mass. He teaches us through the readings. He offers Himself for us to God Our Father. He unites Himself to us in Holy Communion. No wonder we believe that the Holy Mass is our greatest prayer on earth.

Words to Know:

Creed   Gospel   worship

94

THE NICENE CREED

We believe in one God, the Father, the Almighty, Maker of Heaven and earth, of all that is seen and unseen.

We believe in one Lord, Jesus Christ, the only Son of God, eternally begotten of the Father, God from God, Light from Light, true God from true God, begotten, not made, one in Being with the Father. Through Him all things were made. For us men and for our salvation He came down from Heaven: by the power of the Holy Spirit He was born of the Virgin Mary, and became man.

For our sake He was crucified under Pontius Pilate; He suffered, died, and was buried. On the third day He rose again in fulfillment of the Scriptures; He ascended into Heaven and is seated at the right hand of the Father.

He will come again in glory to judge the living and the dead, and His Kingdom will have no end.

We believe in the Holy Spirit, the Lord, the giver of life, Who proceeds from the Father and the Son. With the Father and the Son He is worshipped and glorified. He has spoken through the prophets. We believe in one, holy, Catholic, and apostolic Church. We acknowledge one Baptism for the forgiveness of sins. We look for the resurrection of the dead, and the life of the world to come. *Amen.*

Q. 64 *For what ends is the Sacrifice of the Mass offered?*

The Sacrifice of the Mass is offered for four ends: first, to give supreme honor and glory to God; secondly, to thank Him for all His benefits; thirdly, to satisfy God for our sins and to obtain the grace of repentance; and fourthly, to obtain all other graces and blessings through Jesus Christ.

Q. 65 *Are we obliged to hear Mass?*

We are obliged to hear Mass on Sunday and on the Holy Days of Obligation. But it is good also to attend Mass frequently, in order to participate in the greatest act of religion, the one which is most pleasing to God and most meritorious for us.

Q. 66 *What is the most proper way of attending Mass?*

The most proper way of attending Mass is to offer it to God in union with the priest, reflecting upon the Sacrifice of the Cross, that is, on the Passion, death, and Resurrection of the Lord, and by receiving Holy Communion. For Holy Communion is our actual and real union with the spotless Victim that is offered, and hence the fullest participation in the Holy Sacrifice.

22   Offering Jesus To the Father

After we listen to God's Word and pray the Creed and the Prayer of the Faithful, we prepare our hearts for the most important part of the Mass. This is the moment when Jesus will offer His life to the Father once more through the hands of the priest.

First we must prepare the gifts that go to the altar of God. We call this preparation time the Offertory of the Mass. During the Offertory, bread and wine are taken to the priest. These foods nourish us and keep us alive. By giving them to God, we show that we offer our very lives to Him. We offer Him our hearts. We offer Him all that we think, say, and do. We also offer money in the collection as a sign of our love for His people. All of these gifts are soon to be joined with Jesus, our best gift of all.

Honoring the coming of Jesus, we join with the angels in praising Him: "Holy, holy, holy Lord, God of power and might. Heaven and earth are full of Your glory. Hosanna in the highest. Blessed is He Who comes in the name of the Lord. Hosanna in the highest."

Jesus is now about to come into our midst. The priest bows over the gifts of bread and wine, and says the words of Jesus at the Last Supper. "This is My Body", . . . "This is the Cup of My Blood." This praying over the gifts is called the Consecration. At the moment of Consecration, the bread and wine change into Jesus' Body and Blood. The Host still looks, tastes, and feels like ordinary bread, but it is Jesus, Our Savior. The consecrated wine still looks and tastes like ordinary wine, but it too is Jesus.

The priest takes the Host and lifts it up toward Heaven. We bow our heads because Our Lord is really present before us. The priest

then lifts up the chalice. We bow our heads again. God the Father accepts our offering held up by the priest. As He accepted both the earthly wheat and wine—the work of human hands—now He accepts the consecrated Body and Blood of His own Son, Jesus.

This Consecration is not only the best gift for the Father, it is the greatest treasure we have on earth. It is Jesus Himself among us. The Eucharist is not just a symbol of Jesus, but His real Body, Blood, soul, and divinity. Only the appearance of bread and wine remains. When the priest breaks the Host to eat it, Jesus is fully present in every broken part. If there are any extra consecrated Hosts after the Mass, the priest will treat them with special love and reverence. Once a Host is consecrated, anywhere in the world, it remains the Body, Blood, soul, and divinity of Jesus.

The Consecration of every Holy Mass renews Christ's gift on Calvary. Dying on the Cross, Jesus offered His life to the Father. Now at Mass, His life is offered to the Father through the priest and people of God. Through the Mass, Jesus keeps making up for our sins and uniting us with the Father just as He did in Jerusalem so long ago.

Words to Know:

Eucharist   offertory   Consecration
divinity   appearance   Host

"I will go in to the altar of God, to God Who giveth joy to my youth."

(Psalm 43:4)

Q. 67 *What is the Eucharist?*
The Eucharist is the Sacrament which contains really present the Body, Blood, soul, and divinity of Our Lord Jesus Christ, under the appearances of bread and wine, for the nourishment of souls.

Q. 68 *Is the same Jesus Christ present in the Eucharist Who was born on earth of the Virgin Mary?*
Yes, the same Jesus Christ is present in the Eucharist Who is in Heaven, and Who was born on earth of the Virgin Mary.

Q. 69 *When do the bread and wine become the Body and Blood of Jesus?*
The bread and wine become the Body and Blood of Jesus at the moment of the Consecration.

Q. 70 *After the Consecration, is there nothing left of the bread and the wine?*
After the Consecration, neither bread nor wine is present any longer, but there remain only the "species" or appearances, without their substance.

Q. 71 *When the Host is broken into several parts, is the Body of Jesus Christ broken?*
When the Host is broken into several parts, the Body of Jesus Christ is not broken, but only the appearances of the bread; and the Body of Our Lord remains whole and entire in each of the parts.

Q. 72 *Is Jesus Christ found present in all the consecrated Hosts of the world?*
Yes, Jesus Christ is present in all the consecrated Hosts of the world.

102

23   The Bread of Life

Jesus is the precious gift we offer the Father at Mass. Then we receive Jesus back as a gift into our own souls. In this way, the Sacrifice of the Mass truly forms a bond between Heaven and earth.

As we remember, in the Old Testament, people also offered gifts of value to God. A shepherd and his family might offer up a lamb. The shepherd placed his lamb on an altar and killed it. This was a sign that his gift was completely offered to God. But something else was needed to complete the act of love. The shepherd and his family sat together and ate the lamb as a sacred meal. This was an important sign of their friendship with God. They wanted to be closer to Him by eating something that He had been offered and had accepted.

Under the New Covenant, we lift up the Lamb of God. Then we share in this sacrificial gift by receiving God's own Son in Holy Communion. The priest holds Him before us and says, "This is the Lamb of God Who takes away the sins of the world. Happy are those who are called to His supper." We look at Jesus and answer, "Lord, I am not worthy to receive You, but only say the word and I shall be healed."

The Eucharist really nourishes us. Just as we need food for our bodies to keep us alive, growing, and strong, so we need food for our souls. The Eucharist, the Bread of Life, does this. It keeps the life of grace alive in our hearts. It helps us to grow as good and loving children of God. Jesus said, "Whoever eats of this Bread will never hunger." He also told us that by eating this Bread we will never die; we shall live for ever.

Sharing this sacred banquet unites us in friendship with the Father. It also binds all of us together as one. Our faith in the one, true God makes us a family. All over the world, members of God's family gather to worship the way Jesus taught us at the Last Supper. Whenever we do this in memory of Him, we give joy to the Father. We become more and more like His beloved Son in Whom He is well pleased.

Words to Know:

Communion   worthy

"When we receive the Body of Christ, we share in His life together. We are one because we share one Bread."

(1 Corinthians 10:17)

"As often as you shall eat this Bread and drink the Cup, you proclaim the death of the Lord, until He comes."

(1 Corinthians 11:26)

24 Jesus Comes to Us In the Holy Eucharist

Jesus once changed five loaves and two fishes into food for five thousand people. This miracle of love amazed His followers. But later, Jesus promised them a far more wonderful bread. He explained that this heavenly bread would satisfy the hungers of the heart. Then He told them: "I am the Bread of Life. He who eats My Flesh and drinks My Blood will live for ever."

The Holy Eucharist is the Bread of Life that Jesus promised. We are very fortunate because we can receive it at every Mass. Whenever we do, Jesus comes as a Guest into our hearts.

To prepare for our divine Guest, three things are necessary. We must believe in Him. We must be in His good graces. And we must not eat or drink anything else (except water or medicine) for one hour before He comes to us. These things prepare us properly to receive Holy Communion.

Once we receive Jesus, we kneel down to make a thanksgiving. We may close our eyes to give Him our full attention. We silently pray to Him and He listens. Jesus already knows us completely, but He is pleased when we share our lives with Him. During Holy Communion we can tell Him our disappointments and joys, our hopes and dreams. If we are having trouble being kind or good, Jesus understands. He will help us. If we want to be more obedient at home or school, we can ask Him to show us the way.

Every time Jesus comes to us, He fills our souls with His own life. We become more and more like Him. He gives us the strength to be generous, forgiving, and kind. We become the grace-filled persons God created us to be.

"My Flesh is food indeed, and My Blood is drink indeed. He who eats My Flesh and drinks My Blood, abides in Me and I in him."

(John 6:56—57)

When we love someone, we never get tired of his or her company. We spend as much time with that person as we can. Think of how much more we want to enjoy the company of Jesus. The best way to stay close to Jesus is to go to Mass and receive Holy Communion, even every day if possible. He is the food and life of our souls. If we share in His banquet on earth, He will one day invite us to live with Him for ever in Heaven.

Words to Know:

thanksgiving

"Your fathers ate manna in the desert, and have died. This is the Bread that comes down from Heaven, so that if anyone eat of It, he will not die. I am the Living Bread that has come down from Heaven. If anyone eat of this Bread he shall live for ever; and the Bread that I will give is My Flesh for the life of the world."

(John 6:49—52)

St. Tarcisius

St. Tarcisius was a young Roman boy who lived in the days of the early Christians. Tarcisius secretly learned about Jesus and grew to love Him very much. He started to join the other Christians underground in the catacombs for Mass. Tarcisius especially loved receiving Jesus in Holy Communion. One day the boy was asked to carry the Blessed Sacrament to another Christian who was sick. Tarcisius carefully wrapped the Host in his cloak so it would be safe.

Along the way, Roman boys stopped Tarcisius. "Come play with us", they said. Tarcisius said, "No", and kept walking, protecting the Eucharist close to his heart. "He's carrying something and hiding it from us!" called out one of the children. The boys pulled at Tarcisius' cloak, but he was strong. He would not let go of the Host.

Finally the boys threatened Tarcisius. "If you do not show us what you are hiding, we will throw stones at you." Tarcisius was afraid. But his love for Jesus in the Eucharist was greater than his fear. He accepted death rather than let the sacred Host get into the hands of boys who did not respect or believe in Christ, his Lord.

Let us try to love and believe in Jesus in the Blessed Sacrament just as deeply as did this young boy.

Q. 73 *What things are necessary for the worthy reception of Holy Communion?*
For a worthy reception of Holy Communion three things are necessary: first, to be in the grace of God; second, to realize and to consider Whom we are about to receive; third, to observe the Eucharistic fast.

Q. 74 *Is it a good and useful thing to receive Holy Communion frequently?*
It is a very good thing and most useful to receive Holy Communion frequently, even every day, provided it is done always with the right dispositions.

Q. 75 *What effects does the Eucharist produce in him who receives it worthily?*
In him who receives it worthily, the Holy Eucharist preserves and increases grace, which is the life of the soul, just as food does for the life of the body. The Holy Eucharist takes away venial sins and preserves us from mortal sins, and it gives spiritual joy and consolation by increasing charity and the hope of eternal life of which it is the pledge.

We Pray:

O Sacrament most holy, O Sacrament divine,
All praise and all thanksgiving be every moment Thine.

110

25 Jesus Rises in Splendor

Early on the Sunday morning after Jesus died, some women went to anoint His sacred body with spices and oils. But they arrived to find an empty tomb. The heavy stone that had sealed it was rolled away. And the body of Jesus was nowhere in sight. A beautiful angel told the women Jesus was no longer dead, but alive. "He is risen!" the angel said. "Rejoice and tell the others!"

The women ran to find the apostles and tell them the news. Even though Jesus had told His friends that He would rise on the third day after His death, they were shocked. They wanted to see with their own eyes. Peter and John ran to the tomb and trembled with excitement to see that it was true. Only the burial cloths remained. Jesus had risen from the dead. He was alive!

We are told that the first person to whom Jesus appeared was Mary Magdalen, the holy woman whom He had forgiven many sins. She was weeping in the garden near the tomb because she missed Him. Jesus softly called her by name. She looked up and cried, "Master!" Jesus also appeared to two disciples who were sadly walking in the country. Once the men realized it was Jesus, alive and well, they too raced to tell the apostles.

Soon after, the disciples were all gathered together in an upper room. The doors were locked. Suddenly Jesus appeared! At first, the apostles were afraid Jesus might be a ghost. But Jesus reassured them. "Peace be with you", He said. Then He ate with them. Their joy was great.

Jesus taught us by His life that our suffering and death will be turned into glory and everlasting life. On Good Friday, He suffered and died on the Cross. But on Easter Sunday He arose from the dead in full splendor. Every Easter, we celebrate this miracle of the Resurrection. We rejoice because Jesus' Sacrifice on the Cross destroyed death. Each of us will die one day, but our death will be only a doorway to Heaven. We will be alive for ever just like Jesus, Our Risen Lord.

After He rose from the dead, Jesus stayed among His disciples for forty days. He taught them more about the faith and their mission on earth. He told Peter, the first Pope, to "feed My sheep". He taught all of them to go out to teach and baptize. He promised He would send the Holy Spirit to help them.

Finally it was time for Jesus to go home to Heaven. "I will be with you always, even to the end of time", He promised. Then He rose up into the sky and into glory. Now King of Heaven and earth, Jesus has prepared a place for us in Heaven too. That is why, no matter what happens to us on this earth, we can be full of joy and hope.

"Go, therefore, and make disciples of all nations, baptizing them in the name of the Father, and of the Son, and of the Holy Spirit . . . and, behold, I am with you all days, even until the end of the world."
(Matthew 28:19—20)

Words to Know:

Resurrection   Good Friday   Easter   disciple

The apostle named Thomas doubted Jesus. He was not with the others right after Jesus rose from the dead. He said, "Unless I see in His hands the print of the nails, touch them, and put my finger into His side, I will not believe."

When Jesus appeared in the upper room, He looked straight at Thomas. He said, "Put your finger here; look, here are My hands. Give me your hand; put it into My side, and believe." Thomas did so and then answered in awe, "My Lord and my God."

Jesus said: "Because you have seen Me, you believe. Blessed are those who have not seen, and yet have believed." Jesus was speaking about all of us. One day He will reward us for our faith.

Q. 76 *After His death, what did Jesus Christ do?*
After His death, Jesus Christ descended in His soul to limbo, to the souls of the just who had died up to that time, to take them with Him into Paradise. Then He rose again from the dead, taking up His Body Which had been buried.

Q. 77 *How long did the Body of Jesus Christ remain buried?*
The Body of Jesus Christ remained buried three days, although they were not full days: from Friday evening to the day that we now call Easter Sunday.

Q. 78 *What did Jesus Christ do after His Resurrection?*
After His Resurrection, Jesus Christ remained on earth forty days. Then He ascended to Heaven, where He sits at the right hand of God the Father Almighty.

Q. 79 *Why did Jesus Christ remain on earth forty days after His Resurrection?*
Jesus Christ remained on earth forty days after His Resurrection in order to show that He had really and truly risen from the dead, to confirm His disciples in their faith in Him, and to instruct them more profoundly in His teaching.

Q. 80 *At the present time is Jesus Christ only in Heaven?*

At the present time Jesus Christ is not only in Heaven, but as God He is in every place, and as God-man, He is both in Heaven and in the Most Holy Sacrament of the Altar.

WE PRAY TO GOD AT MASS:

Welcome into Your Kingdom our departed brothers and sisters, and all who have left this world in Your friendship.

116

26 The Coming of The Holy Spirit

After Jesus rose up to Heaven on Ascension Thursday, the apostles prayed and waited with Mary. They all stayed together in one home. Ten days later, a strong wind suddenly swept through the house. A bright flame of fire appeared over each one. These wonderful signs happened as the Holy Spirit came into their hearts, filling them with courage and love.

The people outside heard the wind and gathered to listen. Peter and the other apostles came out of the house in great excitement. They were full of joy and hope. The Holy Spirit created in them such a deep desire to carry on Jesus' work, that they began preaching at once. The Holy Spirit also gave them the power to speak in a way that all people could understand them. Men, women, and children of many countries and languages discovered the Good News that day for the first time.

Peter called out, "Men of Judea and all you who dwell in Jerusalem, hear these words: Jesus of Nazareth was a man sent among you by God. You know this by His miracles, signs, and wonders. God allowed Him to be crucified on a Cross. But now He has raised Him up again. We have seen Him. And now, from Heaven, He has poured out the Holy Spirit as His Father promised."

"The fruit of the Holy Spirit is love, joy, peace, patience, kindness, goodness, and faithfulness."
(Galatians 5:22)

"What must we do?" the people asked. Peter answered, "Repent and be baptized, every one of you, in the name of Jesus Christ for the forgiveness of your sins, and you will receive the gift of the Holy Spirit. This promise is for you and your children, and for all those, everywhere, whom the Lord Our God calls to Himself." That Pentecost Sunday, three thousand people were baptized and the Church was born.

We do not hear a great wind or see tongues of fire, but the Holy Spirit is with us too. He came to live in us on the day we were baptized. That is why we call ourselves temples of the Holy Spirit. We are His dwelling place.

Like the people baptized on Pentecost Sunday, we receive gifts from the Holy Spirit. The Holy Spirit teaches all truth and helps us to understand our lessons about our faith. He inspires us to love others, even when it is hard. He helps us to know and be sorry for our sins. He gives us the grace to be both strong and gentle like Jesus. He is with us always, wherever we go.

Come, Holy Spirit, fill the hearts of Your faithful, and kindle in them the fire of Your love.

Words to Know:

Holy Spirit　　　Pentecost　　　Ascension

"Like mirrors we reflect the glory of the Lord. We grow brighter and brighter as we are changed into the image of Jesus. This is the work of the Holy Spirit."

(adapted from 2 Corinthians 3:18)

SONG OF PRAISE:

Come, Holy Ghost, Creator blest,
And in our hearts take up Your rest.
Come with Your grace and heavenly aid
To fill the hearts which You have made.

120

27 God's Family on Earth

Jesus founded the Church on earth, and He is her King. But before He ascended into Heaven, He asked His apostles to spend the rest of their lives continuing His work. He gave them the power to teach and to forgive sins in His name. He asked them to follow His footsteps in bringing truth, love, and grace into the world.

All of the apostles embraced this mission, but Peter's mission was even greater. One day Jesus told him, "You are Peter and upon this rock I will build My Church. And the gates of Hell shall not prevail against it. I will entrust to you the keys of the Kingdom of Heaven. Whatever you declare bound on earth will be bound in Heaven."

With these words, Jesus invited Peter to take His place on earth. Peter accepted Christ's call. He became the first Pope, the head of the whole Church. Ever since that time, the Church has had an unbroken line of Popes to lead and guide her. We call the Pope the Vicar of Christ because he represents Jesus. Jesus Himself gave him that power. That is why Catholics everywhere respect and obey him.

The Pope is also the head of bishops all over the world. A bishop is like the Good Shepherd that Jesus spoke of in the Gospel. He watches over his flock, protecting it from danger. Today thousands of bishops all over the world carry on the work of the apostles. They teach, preach, and guide. They deliver the message of Jesus. They explain the rules of the Church. They tell us how to avoid sin and lead good lives.

Each bishop has the help of many priests. Priests are very important to the Church because they bring us the grace of the sacraments. They share in the God-given power to forgive sins and offer Holy Mass. We are fortunate to have priests in our parishes, schools, and neighborhoods. Jesus comes into our lives through them.

Other priests bring the light of Christ to faraway parts of the earth. They are joined by religious sisters and brothers who want to give their whole lives to God by teaching and helping others. They are called missionaries. They make the Church rich in blessings by their sacrifices and love.

Bishops, priests, sisters, and brothers are especially called by God to serve the Church. God calls all of us to do special things in the Church too. When we go to Mass every Sunday to pray and worship, we are answering God's call. When we learn about His Word and obey His Commandments, we are serving and loving Him. God wants parents and children and other people in the world to build up His Kingdom just as He calls priests and religious brothers and sisters. We are called the laity of the Church. We are baptized, believing members of God's family.

The laity helps the bishops and priests in bringing the Word of God to all people. Sometimes in doing this work people are asked to offer their lives. We call these persons martyrs. Faith in Christ means so much to them that they risk even death to proclaim it. Jesus said that when men persecute His followers for His name's sake, He will bless His followers with great reward in Heaven.

All of us are destined for Heaven. If we lead a good life on earth, God will take us to be with Him for ever. Members of God's family who have died and now live in Heaven are called saints. The saints were ordinary people, but they loved God with all their hearts and souls. This is the secret of how all of us, no matter what we do in the Church, can become saints.

St. Paul told us that our Church is like a body with many parts. Whenever one small part is hurt, the whole body suffers. For example, we need our eyes to see, our lungs to breathe, and our feet to walk. If any one of these were taken away, our whole body would suffer the loss. So it is with our Church. Christ is the head and we make up all the other parts. Our good actions and prayers build up the health and strength of the whole Church. All of us are one united body under Christ.

This is why the Church is called Catholic. Catholic means "universal" or "for all". Christ founded the Church for everyone. Today because of good priests, missionaries, and lay people, the Church has spread to all nations. Even though we may never see these people in faraway lands, we are one with them because we share the same beliefs. We are all part of God's family on earth—the Catholic Church.

"I am the vine and you are the branches."
(John 15:5)

Words to Know:

the Church   Catholic
religious   missionary   martyr

"If you abide in My Word, you shall be My disciples indeed, and you shall know the truth, and the truth shall make you free."
(John 8:31−32)

Q. 81 *By Whom was the Church founded?*
The Church was founded by Jesus Christ, Who gathered His faithful followers into one society, placed it under the direction of the apostles with St. Peter as its head, and gave it its Sacrifice, its sacraments, and the Holy Spirit Who gives it life.

Q. 82 *Who are the pastors of the Church?*
The pastors of the Church are the Pope and the bishops united with him.

Q. 83 *Who is the Pope?*
The Pope is the successor of St. Peter in the See of Rome and in the Primacy, namely in the universal apostolate and episcopal power. Therefore, he is the visible head of the entire Church, the Vicar of Jesus Christ, Who is the invisible Head; hence, this Church is called the Roman Catholic Church.

28 Our Life in the Church

Signs help us every day of our life. Often they call our attention to important things we cannot see or hear. Smoke is a sign of fire. Red lights or sirens are signs of danger. A rainbow is a sign that we can put our raincoats away because the storm is over.

Signs can also be used to show love. We cannot see love. It is invisible. But love is real, and we can show it to others through our actions. For example, your mother may show you her love by kind words, a hug, or a smile. Hearing, feeling, or seeing these signs helps you to understand the love in your mother's heart. Without signs, her love would be hidden. With signs, you see and understand the wonderful gift that you are receiving.

In the Church, Jesus gave us signs of His grace in the seven sacraments. A sacrament is a sign. It uses things we can see and hear to tell us about something else that we cannot see or hear. Jesus and His grace are hidden from our eyes, but we know He is present in every sacrament. Jesus promised this when He instituted these sacraments during His public life on earth. He wanted to leave us visible signs of His grace being poured out to us.

The first sacrament we receive is Baptism. The signs of this sacrament are words and water. Most of us were baptized when we were little babies. Our parents and godparents took us to Church. They made our baptismal promises for us because we were too young to speak. Then the priest poured water over our heads. He called us by name and said, "I baptize you in the name of the Father, and of the Son, and of the Holy Spirit."

At that very moment, our sin was washed away and our soul was filled with brilliant new life. This new life in our soul was God's own

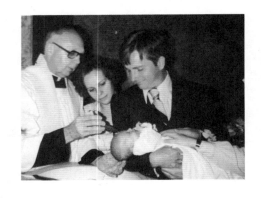

126

life, called grace. God shared grace with us on our Baptism day so that we could be His own precious children for ever. He welcomed us with open arms into His family on earth. Because of our Baptism, He can one day welcome us with open arms into His Kingdom in Heaven.

As a result of our Baptism, we can spend the rest of our life keeping the life of grace alive in our soul. God understands us completely, so He knows that we need special help to do this. That is why He gave us the other sacraments as channels of continuing grace. In this way, He can keep pouring His life and love into our hearts.

In the sacrament of the Holy Eucharist, He gives us His own Son as food for our souls. Bread, wine, and the words of the priest are our signs that Jesus is present. Once the priest changes the bread and wine into Jesus' own Body and Blood, we can receive Him into our hearts. If we receive this sacrament often, the life of grace in our soul grows more and more strong.

In the sacrament of Penance, God gives us the chance to win back grace that we have lost in sin. We know God is really present, because we have the sign of the priest's healing, forgiving words. When he says to us, "Go in peace, your sins are forgiven", Jesus Himself speaks through him, forgiving and blessing us.

When we receive the sacrament of Confirmation, the Holy Spirit fills us with the grace to be even stronger members of the Church. This sacrament will help us to do whatever God asks us as members of His family.

Later in life, we may receive some of the other sacraments: Holy Orders, Matrimony (Marriage), or the Sacrament of the Sick. The important thing to remember is that God gave us the sacraments as a special invitation to share in His life. Receiving them strengthens our friendship with Him and unites us to Him. If we live up to the grace we receive in the sacraments, we really will begin to think, speak, and act like Christ. His own life will shine out of us.

When we are full of God's grace, it is easier to keep our promises to God and follow His Commandments. We love Him so much we want to go to Mass every Sunday, we want to practice our faith and witness it to others. We want to love God most of all, and love our neighbor as ourselves.

Prayer is one of the greatest ways we can show our love of our neighbor. God wants us to pray, not only for those in His family, the Church, but for others who do not have the gift of faith. Jesus told the apostles that He came for everyone. He loves all people. He wants everyone in the world to belong to His family. Even if we cannot join the missionaries in distant lands, we can join them with our prayers. Prayer is powerful, and our prayers for people who do not yet know and love God can bring them closer to Him. Jesus said, "They will know you are My disciples by your love." To be His followers, we must love and pray for all the world.

Words to Know:

sacrament   Christian

". . . Put on love, which binds everything together in perfect harmony. And let the peace of Christ rule in your hearts, to which indeed you were called in the one body."

Colossians 4:14—15

RENEWAL OF BAPTISMAL PROMISES

Do you reject Satan?

I do.

And all his works?

I do.

And all his empty promises?

I do.

Do you reject sin so as to live in the freedom of God's children?

I do.

Do you reject the glamor of evil and refuse to be mastered by sin?

I do.

Do you reject Satan, the father of sin and prince of darkness?

I do.

Do you believe in God, the Father Almighty, the Creator of Heaven and earth?

I do.

Do you believe in Jesus Christ, His only Son, Our Lord, Who was born of the Virgin Mary, was crucified, died, and was buried, rose from the dead and is now seated at the right hand of the Father?

I do.

Do you believe in the Holy Spirit, the Holy Catholic Church, the Communion of Saints, the forgiveness of sins, the resurrection of the body, and life everlasting?

I do.

God, the all-powerful Father of Our Lord Jesus Christ, has given us a new birth by water and the Holy Spirit, and forgiven our sins. May He also keep us faithful to Our Lord Jesus Christ for ever and ever. *Amen.*

Q. 84 *What are the sacraments?*
The sacraments are efficacious signs of grace instituted by Jesus Christ to make us holy.

Q. 85 *How do the sacraments make us holy?*
The sacraments make us holy either by giving us the first sanctifying grace, which takes away sin, or by increasing that grace which we already possess.

Q. 86 *What is Baptism?*
Baptism is the sacrament which makes us Christians, that is, followers of Jesus Christ, sons of God, and members of the Church.

Q. 87 *How is Baptism given?*
Baptism is given by pouring water on the head of the person to be baptized and saying the words of the form at the same time.

29   Mary, Our Mother And Queen

Jesus asked Mary, His own Mother, to be our Mother too, the day she and St. John stood at the foot of His Cross. "Mother," He said, "behold your son. Son, behold your Mother." With that, Mary inherited many, many children—the whole Church!

Mary actually became the Mother of the Church long before that, as a young woman who bravely said "yes" to God's plan. She was free to say "no". But she wanted to do whatever God asked. Because of her trust, obedience, and love, Jesus came into the world as a little Child Who would grow into Our Savior. Mary helped God keep His promise to His people. Her choice brought salvation and light to the world.

God prepared Mary in a very special way for her role in our salvation. He allowed her to be the one person in the world, besides Jesus, who was conceived without original sin. In other words, Mary never needed to be baptized like all of us. We were born with the effects of our first parents' sin. But Mary was born with no trace of sin. That is why she is called the Immaculate Conception. She came into the world already filled with God's life. That is why the angel Gabriel approached her with the words, "Hail Mary, full of grace."

Mary brought Jesus into our world, and she lived her whole life without sin. That is why she holds the highest place after her Son. Just as she brought Jesus to us, so she brings us to Jesus. Sometimes Mary appears on earth with a message from Him. Usually the message is to stop sinning, to love God, and to pray. She tells us these things as a loving Mother, inspiring us gently to be good.

132

We are wise to ask Mary to pray for us, because Jesus always listens to His Mother. His first miracle at the wedding feast in Cana happened at her request. She told Him, "Son, they have no wine." Jesus had not planned to work a miracle that day, but Mary's request won over His heart. He changed six jars of water into delicious wine for the guests of the bride and groom. Just like the couple in Cana, we can go to Mary for help. We can ask her to tell Jesus what we need. Then we can patiently wait for His generous love to answer.

We please God when we try to imitate the virtues of Mary. Mary's greatest desire was to do His will, and she did it in each hour of her life. In Nazareth, she did His will by keeping a happy, comfortable home for Jesus and Joseph. At the foot of the Cross, she did His will in quiet, helpless suffering. After the feast of Pentecost, she did His will by helping the apostles build the early Church.

Now Mary is the Queen of Heaven, but she still does whatever God wills. His will is that she remain a loving Mother in our lives, leading us to Jesus and our heavenly home.

Q. 88 *Was anyone among the descendants of Adam ever preserved from original sin?*
Besides Jesus, Mary alone among the descendants of Adam has been preserved from original sin. Because she was chosen to be the Mother of God, she was "full of grace" (Luke 1:28) and hence free of sin from the first instant of her existence. For this reason the Church celebrates her *Immaculate Conception*.

Words to Know:

Immaculate Conception   full of grace

Our Lady has appeared to her children on earth many times. Each time, she brings a special message to build our hope and faith. In the winter of 1531, Mary appeared in Mexico to a humble man named Juan Diego. In this apparition, we call the Mother of God "Our Lady of Guadalupe". Mary's words to Juan Diego are meant for each one of us:

"Hear me, my dear little child. Let nothing discourage you or make you sad. Do not be afraid of illness, worry, or pain. Am I not here, your Mother? Have I not put you on my lap and sheltered you in my arms? Are you not tucked in the folds of my mantle? Is there anything else you need?"

These words show us that Mary cares for us with the heart of a loving Mother. If we honor and obey her, she will never leave us in this life. She will help us be happy on earth and find our way home to Heaven.

30 The Communion of Saints

Jesus taught us that death is not the end of life, but its real beginning. Death is the doorway to Heaven. Jesus made this possible by His Sacrifice on the Cross. His gift of Himself to the Father was so pleasing that it destroyed death, earning us the right to live for ever. People who live with God in Heaven after they die are called saints. God welcomes the saints into glorious and everlasting happiness.

"Eye has not seen, nor ear heard, nor the heart of man imagined, what God has prepared for those who love Him."

(1 Corinthians 2:9)

While Jesus' death on the Cross won our right to enjoy Heaven, we must do our part to live there one day. The saints earned their heavenly reward. They loved God and kept His laws. They found many ways to know, love, and serve Him during their lives. They were human, so sometimes they sinned or made mistakes. But they came to God, told Him they were sorry, and started all over again. Some of the greatest saints in Heaven, like Mary Magdalen, St. Paul, and St. Augustine, were sinners for a long, long time. But each one finally turned to God and gave Him his whole heart. This love turned them from great sinners into great saints.

136

Many people who love God and die in His friendship are not fully ready for Heaven. First they go to Purgatory to be cleansed of their sins. These souls in Purgatory suffer because they miss God, but the suffering is mixed with joy because they know they will see Him soon. We can help the souls in Purgatory reach Heaven faster by offering our Masses, prayers, and sacrifices for them.

The saints in Heaven, the souls in Purgatory, and the members of the Church on earth make up the whole family of God's people. We call our one great family the Communion of Saints. This Communion of Saints can love and help each other across the barriers of time. Even though the saints are in Heaven, and we are on earth, we can call on them for prayers and help. Even though the souls in Purgatory seem so far away, our prayers make us close to them.

One day this world we live in will come to an end. God will gather all of the people who have ever lived and judge each one. On that day our good actions will be like treasures. God will see them and He will offer us back a crown of glory. Jesus will say, "Come, you who have my Father's blessing. Inherit the Kingdom prepared for you from the beginning of the world!"

We can look forward to this day of rejoicing by preparing our hearts now, today, on earth. We must always keep our eyes and hearts on Heaven because that is our true home. We will get there if we keep knowing, loving, and serving God, our King and final destiny.

"Our hearts are made for You, O Lord, and will not rest until they rest in You."

(St. Augustine)

Q. 89 *What does "Communion of Saints" mean?*
The *Communion of Saints* means that all the faithful who form one single body in Jesus Christ share in all the good that *exists* and *is done* in this same body, namely, in the universal Church.

Words to Know:

Purgatory   Communion of Saints   Last Judgment

WE PRAY TO GOD AT MASS:

There we hope to share in Your glory when every tear will be wiped away. On that day we shall see You, Our God, as You are. We shall become like You and praise You for ever through Christ Our Lord, from Whom all good things come.

Words to Know

Abraham: the father of God's Chosen People.

all-perfect: without fault or defect.

anoint: to put oil on someone as a sign that God is giving His strength or power to that person.

appearance: how something looks.

Ascension: when Jesus went back to Heaven forty days after He rose from the dead.

Baptism: the sacrament which takes away original sin. It gives us God's grace, incorporates us into Christ, and makes us children of God.

bear false witness: to lie about someone.

Bethlehem: the town where Jesus was born.

Bible: the holy book God gave us. It tells about God's love for us, His Chosen People, about the Savior He sent, and about the early days of the Church.

bishop: a man who does the work of the apostles and takes care of a large group of Catholics.

Calvary: the hilltop where Jesus died.

Canaan: the Promised Land God gave to the Israelites.

Catholic: a member of the Catholic Church.

Christian: a baptized follower of Jesus Christ.

Church, the: the group of followers of Jesus who believe the same faith, receive the sacraments, and obey the Pope; another name for the family of God.

Commandment: a law of God.

Communion: *see* Eucharist.

Communion of Saints: the unity of all the members of the Church here on earth with those in Heaven and in Purgatory.

Consecration: the part of the Mass when the priest changes the bread and wine into the Body and Blood of Jesus.

contrition: sorrow for sin.

Covenant: a contract or agreement between two or more persons or groups. God made a Covenant with the Israelites, His Chosen People.

covet: wrongfully to desire something which does not belong to you.

create: to make something out of nothing.

Creator: God, the Maker of all things.

Creed: a prayer telling what we believe.

David: the boy who killed Goliath and grew up to be a king of Israel. Jesus descended from the family of David.

disciple: a follower of Jesus.

divinity: the nature of God.

Easter: the day on which Jesus rose from the dead.

Eucharist: the sacrament in which Jesus comes to us in the appearance of bread and wine; the Body and Blood of Jesus.

examination of conscience: thinking about what we did to see if it was good or bad in preparation for confession.

faith: a gift from God by which we believe in Him and everything He teaches us.

Fall, the: the sin of our first parents, Adam and Eve.

forgiveness: the act of pardoning someone who has done something wrong.

foster father: a man who takes the place of the real father.

full of grace: all holy, being free from sin. This was the angel's greeting to Mary.

Goliath: a gigantic Philistine soldier whom David killed.

Good Friday: the day Jesus suffered and died for us.

good will: always wanting to do what is right.

140

Gospel: the "Good News"; the story of the life, death, and Resurrection of Jesus.

grace: the life of God in our souls. We receive grace from the sacraments, from prayer, and from doing good works.

Heaven: the place of perfect happiness with God for ever. Heaven is for those who have asked God to forgive their sins and who have died in His love.

Holy Day of Obligation: a special feast day, besides Sunday, when Catholics are required to participate at Mass and not do unnecessary work.

Holy Thursday: the day Jesus gave us the Holy Eucharist for the first time.

Holy Spirit: God, the Third Person of the Holy Trinity.

honesty: truthfulness.

honor: to love, respect, and obey.

Host: the round wafer of bread used at Mass. At the Consecration it is changed into Jesus, the Bread of Life.

humble: not proud.

Immaculate Conception: the special gift God gave to the Blessed Virgin Mary of being free from original sin from the first moment of her life.

infinite: perfect, without end.

John the Baptist: a cousin of Jesus. John was the last of the prophets. He helped prepare the people for the coming of Jesus.

king: a ruler.

Last Judgment: the event at the end of the world at which God will judge our lives.

Last Supper: the dinner Jesus had with the Twelve Apostles the night before He died. At the Last Supper Jesus gave us the Holy Eucharist.

Lord: a name for Jesus because He is the King of the universe.

manger: a box that holds feed for animals.

martyr: a person who dies for his faith in Jesus.

Mass: the Sacrifice of Jesus on the Cross offered by the priest in our church and in every Catholic church.

miracle: something wonderful that is done by the power of God and that only God can do.

missionary: a person who works to spread the Good News of Jesus in every part of the world.

mortal sin: a very big sin that kills all life of grace in a soul.

Moses: a leader and prophet of the Israelites; God gave the people Ten Commandments through him.

Mount Sinai: the mountain on which God made a Covenant with the Israelites and gave the Ten Commandments.

New Testament: the second part of the Holy Bible. It tells us about the life and teachings of Jesus and the early Church.

obey: to do what we are told.

Offertory: the part of the Mass where bread and wine are brought to the altar and offered as a gift to God.

Old Testament: the first part of the Holy Bible. It tells the history and preparation of God's chosen people for the coming of the Savior.

original sin: the first sin, committed when Adam and Eve disobeyed God. We are all born with original sin on our souls.

parable: a story that teaches a lesson.

Passion: the suffering and death of Jesus to free us from sin.

penance: a prayer we say or something we do to help make up for our sins.

Pentecost: the coming of the Holy Spirit to the apostles.

Pharaoh: a ruler in ancient Egypt.

142

Pope: the chief leader and teacher of the Catholic Church who takes the place of Jesus on earth.

prayer: the lifting of the heart and mind to God; talking with God.

prophet: a man who prepared the people for the coming of the Savior.

Purgatory: the place where a soul goes to be made clean from all venial sin and receive the punishment due to sins already forgiven before it can go to Heaven.

purity: cleanness in thought, word, and act.

redeem: to buy back; to free someone by buying freedom for him.

religious: men and women who are dedicated to God in a special way.

remembrance: in memory of someone or something.

respect: to think highly of.

Resurrection: when Jesus rose from the dead.

reverent: showing respect.

sacrament: a sign given by Jesus that gives us grace.

sacrament of Penance: the sacrament in which all sins committed after Baptism are forgiven; also called Confession or Reconciliation.

sacrifice: something that is offered to God. At Mass we offer Jesus to God the Father as a sacrifice for our sins.

saint: a holy person who loved God very much on earth and now is in Heaven.

Savior: Jesus Christ, who died to save us all from sin.

sin: any wrong we do on purpose. Sin turns us away from God.

sorrow for sins: feeling sorry for what we have done.

stable: a place where farm animals eat and sleep.

superstition: thinking that ordinary things have powers that only God has.

Temple: the building in Jerusalem where the Jews worshipped God.

thanksgiving: giving thanks.

trust: to depend on or hope in.

truth: the way things actually are.

venial sin: a small sin that makes a soul weak and less pleasing to God.

vow: a free promise we make to God.

worship: love, honor, and adoration which we give to God.

worthy: having value, being deserving.

We Pray

THE SIGN OF THE CROSS

In the Name of the Father, and of the Son, and of the Holy Spirit. *Amen.*

OUR FATHER

Our Father, Who art in Heaven, hallowed be Thy Name; Thy Kingdom come; Thy will be done on earth as it is in Heaven. Give us this day our daily bread, and forgive us our trespasses as we forgive those who trespass against us; and lead us not into temptation, but deliver us from evil. *Amen.*

HAIL MARY

Hail Mary, full of grace! The Lord is with thee. Blessed art thou among women, and blessed is the fruit of thy womb, Jesus. Holy Mary, Mother of God, pray for us sinners, now and at the hour of our death. *Amen.*

GLORY BE

Glory be to the Father, and to the Son, and to the Holy Spirit, as it was in the beginning, is now, and ever shall be, world without end. *Amen.*

MORNING OFFERING

O my God, I offer You every thought and word and act of today. Please bless me, my God, and make me good today. *Amen.*

APOSTLES' CREED

I believe in God, the Father Almighty, Creator of Heaven and earth, and in Jesus Christ, His only Son, Our Lord, Who was conceived by the Holy Spirit, born of the Virgin Mary, suffered under Pontius Pilate, was crucified, died, and was buried. He descended into Hell; the third day He rose again from the dead. He ascended into Heaven and sits at the right hand of God, the Father Almighty; from thence He shall come to judge the living and the dead. I believe in the Holy Spirit, the Holy Catholic Church, the Communion of Saints, the forgiveness of sins, the resurrection of the body, and life everlasting. *Amen.*

ACT OF CONTRITION

O my God, I am heartily sorry for having offended You. I detest all my sins because of Your just punishments, but most of all because they offend You, my God, Who are all-good and deserving of all my love. I firmly resolve, with the help of Your grace, to confess my sins, to do penance, and to amend my life. *Amen.*

PRAYER TO THE GUARDIAN ANGEL

Angel of God, my guardian dear, To whom God's love commits me here, Ever this day be at my side, To light and guard, to rule and guide. *Amen.*

STATIONS OF THE CROSS

1. Jesus is condemned to death.
2. Jesus carries His Cross.
3. Jesus falls the first time.
4. Jesus meets His Mother.
5. Jesus is helped by Simon.
6. Veronica wipes the face of Jesus.
7. Jesus falls a second time.
8. Jesus speaks to the women.
9. Jesus falls a third time.
10. Jesus is stripped of His clothes.
11. Jesus is nailed to the Cross.
12. Jesus dies on the Cross.
13. Jesus is taken down from the Cross.
14. Jesus is placed in the tomb.

EXAMINATION OF CONSCIENCE

How have I acted toward God? Do I think of God and speak to Him by praying to Him each day?

Do I speak of God with reverence?

Do I go to Mass on Sunday?

Do I do all I can to make Sunday a day of rest and joy for my family?

Do I participate in Mass, or do I tease or distract others by laughing, talking, or playing?

Do I pay attention to my parents, priests, and teachers when they talk to me about God?

How have I acted toward others?

Do I obey my parents and teachers quickly and cheerfully, or must I be reminded many times?

Do I tell my parents or those in authority over me that I am sorry and ask them to forgive me when I have not minded them?

Do I obey the rules of my home and school?

Do I help my brothers, sisters, and classmates when they need my help?

Am I kind to everyone?

Did I hit, kick, or in any way hurt others on purpose?

Am I willing to play with everyone?

Did I make fun or say mean things to anyone?

Do I do all my classwork and my chores at home well?

Do I take care of my health by eating the right food, etc.?

Do I think or do bad things or say bad words?

Do I tell the truth?

Do I say things about other people that are not true?

Did I cheat in class or in a game?
Did I steal or keep things that are not mine?
Am I willing to share my things with others?
Do I return things that I have borrowed?

Art Credits

page   ART RESOURCE, NEW YORK:

cover   *The Raising of Lazarus* (detail), Fra Angelico (Scala)

  12   *Creation of the Animals*, Rouen (Giraudon)
  16   *Baptism of Christ* (detail), Perugino (Scala)
  24   *The Sacrifice of Isaac*, Tiepolo (SEF)
  34   *Breaking the Tablets of the Law* (detail), Rosselli (Scala)
  38   *Angels in Adoration* (detail), Gozzoli (Scala)
  52   *Annunciation* (detail), Filippo Lippi (Scala)
  58   *Road to Calvary* (detail), Tintoretto (Scala)
  72   *St. John Baptizing Christ* (detail), Ghirlandaio (Scala)
  80   *The Last Supper*, D. Bouts (Giaudon)
  88   *Deposition* (detail), Fra Bartolomeo (Nimatallah)
102   *Christ Giving Communion to the Apostles*, Fra Angelico (Scala)
110   *Noli Me Tangere*, Duccio (Scala)
120   *St. Augustine and Child* (detail), Pinturicchio (Scala)
136   *The Tribune*, Sainte Chapelle (Scala)

NATIONAL GALLERY OF ART, WASHINGTON, D.C.:

  26   *The Finding of Moses* (detail), Sebastien Bourdon; Samuel H. Kress Collection
  30   *The Youthful David*, Andrea del Castagno; Widener Collection
  66   *The Adoration of the Shepherds*, Giorgione; Samuel H. Kress Collection
  74   *The Marriage at Cana*, Master of the Retable of the Reyes Catolicos; Samuel H. Kress Collection
  84   *The Crucifixion with St. Jerome and St. Francis*, Pesellino; Samuel H. Kress Collection
132   *The Assumption of the Virgin*, Michael Sittow; Ailsa Mellon Bruce Fund

METROPOLITAN MUSEUM OF ART, NEW YORK

   6   *God the Father*, Raphael (lunette from *Madonna and Child Enthroned with Saints*); gift of J. Pierpont Morgan, 1916

NATIONAL GALLERY OF IRELAND, DUBLIN

116   *The Descent of the Holy Spirit*, Bartholome Zeitbolm

HISPANIC SOCIETY OF AMERICA, NEW YORK

46   *The Holy Family*, Morales

PHOTOGRAPHS:

Gary Fuchs: 20 (Expulsion from the Garden of Eden, Palermo); other photos: pp.
44, 62, 92, 98, 106, 126 (Confession and Eucharist)
Nacelewicz: 126 (Baptism)
Diocese of Wichita: 126 (Confirmation)
McCaffrey: 126 (Marriage)
Oblates of the Blessed Virgin Mary, Boston: 126 (Ordination)
J. Monti: 126 (Anointing)